DUTCH AND ENGLISH ON THE HUDSON

TEXTBOOK EDITION

∵

THE CHRONICLES
OF AMERICA SERIES
ALLEN JOHNSON
EDITOR

GERHARD R. LOMER
CHARLES W. JEFFERYS
ASSISTANT EDITORS

DUTCH AND ENGLISH
ON THE HUDSON

A CHRONICLE OF
COLONIAL NEW YORK
BY MAUD WILDER GOODWIN

NEW HAVEN: YALE UNIVERSITY PRESS
TORONTO: GLASGOW, BROOK & CO.
LONDON: HUMPHREY MILFORD
OXFORD UNIVERSITY PRESS

PRINTED IN THE UNITED STATES OF AMERICA

12457

CONTENTS

DUTCH AND ENGLISH ON THE HUDSON

∴

CHAPTER I

UP THE GREAT RIVER

GEOGRAPHY is the maker of history. The course
of Dutch settlement in America was predeter-
mined by a river which runs its length of a hundred
and fifty miles from the mountains to the sea
through the heart of a fertile country and which
offers a natural highway for transportation of
merchandise and for communication between colonies. No man, however, could foresee the development of the Empire State when, on that
memorable September day in 1609, a small Dutch
yacht named the *Halve Maene* or *Half Moon*, under
the command of Captain Henry Hudson, slipped
in past the low hook of sand in front of the
Navesink Heights, and sounded her way to an

anchorage in what is now the outer harbor of New York.

Robert Juet of Limehouse, one of the adventurers sailing with Hudson, writes in his journal:

At three of the clock in the afternoone we came to three great rivers, so we stood along to the northermost, thinking to have gone into it; but we found it to have a very shoald barre before it, for we had but ten foot water; then wee cast about to the southward and found two fathoms, three fathoms, and three and a quarter, till we came to the souther side of them; then we had five and sixe fathoms and anchored. So wee sent in our boate to sound and they found no lesse water than foure, five, six, and seven fathoms and returned in an hour and a half. So wee weighed and went in and rode in five fathoms, oozie ground, and saw many salmons, mullets and rayes very great.

So quietly is chronicled one of the epoch-making events of history, an event which opened a rich territory and gave to the United Netherlands their foothold in the New World, where Spain, France, and England had already established their claims.

Let us try to call to our minds the picture of the *Half Moon* as she lies there in harbor, a quaint, clumsily built boat of forty lasts, or eighty tons, burden. From her bow projects a beakhead, a sort of gallery, painted and carved, and used as a place of rest or of punishment for the sailors. At the tip of the beakhead is the figurehead, a red lion with a golden mane. The ship's bow is green, with ornaments of sailors' heads painted red and yellow. Both forecastle and poop are high, the latter painted a blue mottled with white clouds. The stern below is rich in color and carving. Its upper panels show a blue ground picked out with stars and set in it a crescent holding a profile of the traditional Man in the Moon. The panel below bears the arms of the City of Amsterdam and the letters V. O. C. forming the monogram of the Dutch East India Company — Vereenigde Oost-Indische Compagnie.

Five carved heads uphold the stern, above which hangs one of those ornate lanterns which the Dutch love so well. To add to all this wealth of color, flags are flying from every masthead. At the foretop flutters the tricolor of red, white, and black, with the arms of Amsterdam in a field of white. At the maintop flames the flag of the seven provinces of the Netherlands, emblazoned with a red lion rampant, bearing in his paws a sword and seven arrows. The bowsprit bears a small flag of orange, white, and blue, while from the stern flies the Dutch East India Company's special banner. It is no wonder that such an apparition causes the simple natives ashore to believe first that some marvelous bird has swept in from the sea, and then that a mysterious messenger from the Great Spirit has appeared in all his celestial robes.

If Hudson's object had been stage-setting for the benefit of the natives, he could not have arranged his effects better. The next day, when the ship had moved to a good harbor, the people of the country were allowed to come aboard to barter "greene Tabacco" for knives and beads. Hudson probably thought that the savages might learn a lesson in regard to the power of the newcomers by an inspection of the interior of the ship. The cannon which protruded their black noses amidships held their threat of destruction even when they were not belching thunder and lightning. The forecastle with its neatly arranged berths must have seemed a strange contrast to the bare ground on which the savages were accustomed to sleep, and the brightness of polished and engraved brass tablets caught the untutored eyes which could not decipher the inscriptions. There were three of these tablets, the mottoes of which, being translated, read: *Honor thy father and thy mother! Do not fight without cause! Good advice makes the wheels run smoothly!*

Perhaps the thing which interested the Indians most was the great wooden block fastened to the deck behind the mainmast. This strange object was fashioned in the shape of a man's head, and through it passed the ropes used to hoist the yards. It was called sometimes "the silent servant," sometimes "the knighthead." To the Indians it must have seemed the final touch of necromancy, and they were prepared to bow down in awe before a race of beings who could thus make blocks of wood serve them.

Trusting, no doubt, to the impression which he had made on the minds of the natives, Hudson decided to go ashore. The Indians crowded around him and "sang in their fashion" — a motley horde, as strange to the ship's crew as the *Half Moon* and its company seemed marvelous to the aborigines. Men, women, and children, dressed in fur or tricked out with feathers, stood about or floated in their boats hewn from solid logs, the men carrying pipes of red copper in which they smoked that precious product, tobacco — the consolation prize offered by the New World to the Old in lieu of the hoped-for passage to Cathay.

Everything seemed to breathe assurance of peaceful relations between the red man and the white; but if the newcomers did not at the moment realize the nature of the Indians, their eyes were opened to possibilities of treachery by the happenings of the next day. John Colman and a boat's crew were sent out to take further soundings before the *Half Moon* should proceed on her journey. As the boat was returning to report a safe course ahead, the crew, only five in number, were set upon by two war-canoes filled with Indians, whose volley of arrows struck terror to their hearts. Colman was mortally wounded in the throat by an arrow, and two of his companions were seriously, though not fatally, hurt. Keeping up a running fight, the survivors escaped under cover of darkness. During the night, as they crouched with their dead comrade in the boat, the sailors must have thought the minutes hours and the hours days. To add to their discomfort rain was falling, and they drifted forlornly at the mercy of the current. When at last dawn came, they could make out the ship at a great distance; but it was ten o'clock in the morning before they reached her safe shelter. So ended the brief dream of ideal friendship and confidence between the red men and the whites

After Colman had been buried in a grave by the side of the beautiful sheet of water which he had known for so short a time, the *Half Moon* worked her way cautiously from the Lower Bay through the Narrows to the inner harbor and reached the tip of the island which stands at its head. What is now a bewildering mass of towers and palaces of industry, looking down upon a far-extended fleet of steam and sailing vessels, was then a point, wooded to the water's edge, with a scattered Indian village nestling among the trees.

A Moravian missionary, writing at the beginning of the nineteenth century, set down an account from the red man's point of view of the arrival of the *Half Moon*. This account he claimed to have received from old Indians who held it as part of their tribal traditions. As such it is worth noting and quoting, although as history it is of more than doubtful authenticity. The tradition runs that the chiefs of the different tribes on sighting the *Half Moon* supposed it to be a supernatural visitor and assembled on " York Island " to deliberate on the manner in which they should receive this Manito on his arrival. Plenty of meat was provided for a sacrifice, a grand dance was arranged, and the medicine-men were set to work to determine the meaning of this phenomenon. The runners sent out to observe and report declared it certain that it was the Great Manito, "but other runners soon after arriving, declare it a large house of various colors, full of people yet of quite a different color than they [the Indians] are of. That they were also dressed in a different manner from them and that one in particular appeared altogether red, which must be the Mannitto himself."

The strange craft stopped and a smaller boat drew near. While some stayed behind to guard the boat, the red-clothed man with two others advanced into a large circle formed by the Indian chiefs and wise men. He saluted them and they returned the salute.

A large hock-hack [Indian for gourd or bottle] is brought forward by the supposed Mannitto's servants and from this a substance is poured out into a small cup or glass and handed to the Mannitto. The expected Mannitto drinks, has the glass filled again and hands it to the chief next him to drink. The chief receives the glass but only smelleth at it and passes it on to the next chief who does the same. The glass then passes through the circle without the contents being tasted by anyone, and is upon the point of being returned again to the red-clothed man when one of their number, a spirited man and a great warrior jumps up and harangues the assembly on the impropriety of returning the glass with the contents in it — that the same was handed them by the Mannitto in order that they should drink it as he himself had done before them — that this would please him; but that to return it might provoke him and be the cause of their being destroyed by him. He then took the glass and bidding the assembly a farewell, drank it up. Every eye was fixed on their resolute companion to see what an effect this would have upon him and he soon beginning to stagger about and at last dropping to the ground they bemoan him. He falls into a sleep and they saw him as expiring. He awakes again, jumps up and declares that he never felt himself before so happy as after he had drank the cup. Wishes for more. His wish is granted and the whole assembly soon join him and become intoxicated.

The Delawares, as the missionary points out further, call New York Island "Mannahattanik," "the place where we were all drunk." With this picturesque account let us contrast the curt statement of Robert Juet: "This morning at our first rode in the River there came eight and twenty canoes full of men, women and children to betray us; but we saw their intent and suffered none of them to come aboord of us. At twelve of the clocke they departed. They brought with them oysters and beanes whereof we bought some." If there had been any such striking scene as the missionary's chronicle reports, Juet would probably have recorded it; but in addition to his silence in the matter we must recall the fact that this love-feast is supposed to have occurred only a few days after the killing of Colman and the return of the terror-stricken crew. This makes it seem extremely improbable that Hudson would have taken the risk of going ashore among hostile natives and proffering the hospitalities which had been so ill requited on his previous landing. Let us therefore pass by the Reverend John Heckwelder's account as "well found, but not well founded," and continue to follow the cruise of the *Half Moon* up the great river.

The days now were fair and warm, and Hudson, looking around him when the autumn sun had swept away the haze from the face of the water, declared it as fair a land as could be trodden by the foot of man. He left Manhattan Island behind, passed the site of Yonkers, and was carried by a southeasterly wind beyond the Highlands till he reached what is now West Point. In this region of the Catskills the Dutch found the natives friendly, and, having apparently recovered from their first suspicious attitude, the explorers began to open barter and exchange with such as wished to come aboard. On at least one occasion Hudson himself went ashore. The early Dutch writer, De Laet, who used Hudson's last journal, quotes at length Hudson's description of this landing, and the quotation, if genuine, is probably the longest description of his travels that we have from the pen of the great navigator. He says that he sailed to the shore in one of their canoes, with an old man who was chief of a tribe. There he found a house of oak bark, circular in shape, apparently well built, and with an arched roof.

On our coming near the house, two mats were spread to sit upon and immediately some food was served in well-made red wooden bowls; two men were also dispatched at once with bows and arrows in quest of game, who soon after brought a pair of pigeons which they had shot. They likewise killed at once a fat dog and skinned it in great haste, with shells which they get out of the water. . . . The natives are a very good people, for when they saw that I would not remain, they supposed that I was afraid of their bows, and taking the arrows they broke them in pieces and threw them into the fire.

So the *Half Moon* drifted along "*the River of the Steep Hills,*" through the golden autumnal weather, now under frowning cliffs, now skirting low sloping shores and fertile valleys, till at length the shoaling water warned Hudson that he could not penetrate much farther. He knew now that he had failed to find the northwest passage to Cathay which had been the object of his expedition; but he had explored one of the world's noblest rivers from its mouth to the head of its navigable waters.

It is a matter of regret to all students that so little is known of this great adventurer. Sober history tells us that no authentic portrait of him is extant; but I like to figure him to myself as drawn by that mythical chronicler, Diedrich Knicker-bocker, who was always ready to help out fact with fiction and both with humor. He pictures Henry Hudson as "a short, brawny old gentleman with a double chin, a mastiff mouth and a broad copper nose which was supposed in those days to have acquired its fiery hue from the constant neighborhood of his tobacco pipe. He wore a true Andrea Ferrara, tucked in a leathern belt, and a commodore's cocked hat on one side of his head. He was remarkable for always jerking up his breeches when he gave his orders and his voice sounded not unlike the brattling of a tin trumpet, owing to the number of hard northwesters which he had swallowed in the course of his sea-faring."

This account accords with our idea of this doughty navigator far better than the popular picture of the forlorn white-bearded old gentleman amid the arctic ice-floes. The cause of the fiery nose seems more likely to have been spirits than tobacco, for Hudson was well acquainted with the effects of strong waters. At one stage of his journey he was responsible for an incident which may perhaps have given rise to the Indian legend of the mysterious potations attending the first landing of the white men. Hudson invited certain native chiefs to the ship and so successfully plied them with brandy that they were completely intoxicated. One fell asleep and was deserted by his comrades, who, however, returned next day and were rejoiced to find the victim professing great satisfaction over his experience.

The ship had now reached the northernmost bounds of her exploration and anchored at a point not exactly determined but not far below Albany. Hudson sent an exploring boat a little farther, and on its return he put the helm of the *Half Moon* about and headed the red lion with the golden mane southward. On this homeward course, the adventurers met with even more exciting experiences than had marked their progress up the river. At a place near the mouth of Haverstraw Bay at Stony Point the *Half Moon* was becalmed and a party of Mountain Indians came off in canoes to visit the ship. Here they showed the cunning and the thieving propensities of which Hudson accused them, for while some engaged the attention of the crew on deck, one of their number ran his canoe under the stern and contrived to climb by the aid of the rudder-post into the cabin.

To understand how this theft was carried out it is necessary to remember the build of the seventeenth century Dutch sailing-vessels in which the forecastle and poop rose high above the waist of the ship. In the poop were situated the cabins of the captain and the mate. Of Hudson's cabin we have a detailed description. Its height was five feet three inches. It was provided with lockers, a berth, a table, and a bench with four divisions, a most desirable addition when the vessel lurched suddenly. Under the berth were a box of books and a medicine-chest, besides such other equipment as a globe, a compass, a silver sun-dial, a cross staff, a brass tinder-box, pewter plates, spoons, a mortar and pestle, and the half-hour glass which marked the different watches on deck.

Doubtless the savage intruder would have been glad to capture some of this rich booty; but it must have been the mate's cabin into which he stumbled, for he obtained only a pillow and a couple of shirts, for which he sold his life. The window in the stern projecting over the water was evidently standing open in order to admit the soft September air, and the Indian saw his chance. Into this window he crept and from it started to make off with the stolen goods; but the mate saw the thief, shot, and killed him. Then all was a scene of wild confusion. The savages scattered from the ship, some taking to their canoes, some plunging into the river. The small boat was sent in pursuit of the stolen goods, which were soon recovered; but, as the boat returned, a red hand reached up from the water to upset it, whereupon the ship's cook, seizing a sword, cut off the hand as it gripped the gunwale, and the wretched owner sank never to reappear.

On the following day Hudson and his men came into conflict with more than a hundred savages, who let loose a flight of arrows. But one of the ship's cannon was trained upon them, and one shot followed by a discharge of musketry quickly ended the battle. The mariners thereupon made their way without molestation to the mouth of the river, whence they put to sea on a day in early October, only a month after their entrance into the bay.

Hudson was destined never again to see the

country from which he set out on this quest, never again to enter the river which he had explored. But he had achieved immortal fame for himself and had secured a new empire for the Netherlands. The Cabots possibly, and Verrazano almost certainly, had visited the locality of "the Great River" before him; but Hudson was in the truest sense its discoverer, and history has accorded him his rights. Today the replica of the *Half Moon* lies in a quiet backwater of the Hudson River at the foot of Bear Mountain — stripped of her gilding, her sails, and her gay pennants. She still makes a unique appeal to our imagination as we fancy the tiny original buffeting the ocean waves and feeling her way along uncharted waters to the head of navigation. To see even the copy is to feel the thrill of adventure and to realize the boldness of those early mariners whom savages could not affright nor any form of danger daunt.[1]

[1] For further details of the appearance of the *Half Moon*, see E. H. Hall's paper on *Henry Hudson and the Discovery of the Hudson River*, published by the American Scenic and Historic Preservation Society (1910).

CHAPTER II

As he was returning to Holland from his voyage to
America, Hudson was held with his ship at the
port of Dartmouth, on the ground that, being an
Englishman by birth, he owed his services to his
country. He did not again reach the Netherlands,
but he forwarded to the Dutch East India Company a report of his discoveries. Immediately the
enthusiasm of the Dutch was aroused by the pros-
pect of a lucrative fur trade, as Spain had been set
aflame by the first rumors of gold in Mexico and
Peru; and the United Provinces, whose indepen-
dence had just been acknowledged, thereupon laid
claim to the new country.

To a seafaring people like the Dutch, the ocean
which lay between them and their American
possessions had no terrors, and the twelve-year
truce just concluded with Spain set free a vast
energy to be applied to commerce and oversea

trading. Within a year after the return of the *Half Moon*, Dutch merchants sent out a second ship, the crew of which included several sailors who had served under Hudson and of which the command was given, in all probability, to Hudson's former mate. The vessel was soon followed by the *Fortune*, the *Tiger*, the *Little Fox*, and the *Nightingale*. By this time the procession of vessels plying between the Netherlands Old and New was fairly set in motion. But the aim of all these voyages was commerce rather than colonization. Shiploads of tobacco and furs were demanded by the promoters, and to obtain these traders and not farmers were needed.

The chronicle of these years is melancholy reading for lovers of animals, for never before in the history of the continent was there such a wholesale, organized slaughter of the unoffending creatures of the forest. Beavers were the greatest sufferers. Their skins became a medium of currency, and some of the salaries in the early days of the colony were paid in so many "beavers." The manifest of one cargo mentions 7246 beavers, 675 otters, 48 minks, and 36 wildcats.

In establishing this fur trade with the savages, the newcomers primarily required trading-posts guarded by forts. Late in 1614 or early in 1615, therefore, Fort Nassau was planted on a small island a little below the site of Albany. Here the natives brought their peltries and the traders unpacked their stores of glittering trinkets, knives, and various implements of which the Indians had not yet learned the use. In 1617 Fort Nassau was so badly damaged by a freshet that it was allowed to fall into ruin, and later a new stronghold and trading-post known as Fort Orange was set up where the city of Albany now stands.

Meanwhile in 1614 the States-General of the United Netherlands had granted a charter to a company of merchants of the city of Amsterdam, authorizing their vessels "exclusively to visit and navigate" the newly discovered region lying in America between New France and Virginia, now first called New Netherland. This monopoly was limited to four voyages, commencing on the first of January, 1615, or sooner. If any one else traded in this territory, his ship and cargo were liable to confiscation and the owners were subject to a heavy fine to be paid to the New Netherland Company. The Company was chartered for only three years, and at the expiration of the time a renewal of the charter was refused, although the

Company was licensed to trade in the territory from year to year.

In 1621 this haphazard system was changed by the granting of a charter which superseded all private agreements and smaller enterprises by the incorporation of "that great armed commercial association," the Dutch West India Company. By the terms of the charter the States-General engaged to secure to the Company freedom of traffic and navigation within prescribed limits, which included not only the coast and countries of Africa from the Tropic of Cancer to the Cape of Good Hope but also the coasts of America. Within these vague and very extended bounds the Company was empowered to make contracts and alliances, to build forts, to establish government, to advance the peopling of fruitful and unsettled parts, and to "do all that the service of those countries and the profit and increase of trade shall require."

For these services the States-General agreed to grant a subsidy of a million guilders, or about half a million dollars, "provided that we with half the aforesaid million of guilders, shall receive and bear profit and risk in the same manner as the other members of this Company." In case of war, which was far from improbable at this time, when the twelve years' truce with Spain was at an end, the Company was to be assisted, if the situation of the country would in any wise admit of it, "with sixteen warships and four yachts, fully armed and equipped, properly mounted, and provided in all respects both with brass and other cannon and a proper quantity of ammunition, together with double suits of running and standing rigging, sails, cables, anchors, and other things thereto belonging, such as are proper to be used in all great expeditions." These ships were to be manned, victualed, and maintained at the expense of the Company, which in its turn was to contribute and maintain sixteen like ships of war and four yachts.

The object of forming this great company with almost unlimited power was twofold, at once political and commercial. Its creators planned the summoning of additional military resources to confront the hostile power of Spain and also the more thorough colonization and development of New Netherland. In these purposes they were giving expression to the motto of the House of Nassau: "I will maintain."

Two years elapsed between the promulgation of the charter and the first active operations of the

West India Company; but throughout this period the air was electric with plans for occupying and settling the new land beyond the sea. Finally in March, 1623, the ship *Nieu Nederlandt* sailed for the colony whose name it bore, under the command of Cornelis Jacobsen May, of Hoorn, the first Director-General. With him embarked some thirty families of Walloons, who were descendants of Protestant refugees from the southern provinces of the Netherlands, which, being in general attached to the Roman Catholic Church, had declined to join the confederation of northern provinces in 1579. Sturdy and industrious artisans of vigorous Protestant stock, the Walloons were a valuable element in the colonization of New Netherland. After a two months' voyage the ship *Nieu Nederlandt* reached the mouth of the Hudson, then called the Mauritius in honor of the Stadholder, Prince Maurice, and the leaders began at once to distribute settlers with a view to covering as much country as was defensible. Some were left in Manhattan, several families were sent to the South River, now the Delaware, others to Fresh River, later called the Connecticut, and others to the western shore of Long Island. The remaining colonists, led by Adriaen Joris, voyaged up the length of the Mauritius, landed at Fort Orange, and made their home there. Thus the era of settlement as distinguished from trade had begun.

The description of the first settlers at Wiltwyck, on the western shore of the great river, may be applied to all the pioneer Dutch colonists. "Most of them could neither read nor write. They were a wild, uncouth, rough, and most of the time a drunken crowd. They lived in small log huts, thatched with straw. They wore rough clothes, and in the winter were dressed in skins. They subsisted on a little corn, game, and fish. They were afraid of neither man, God, nor the Devil. They were laying deep the foundation of the Empire State."[1]

The costume of the wife of a typical settler usually consisted of a single garment, reaching from neck to ankles. In the summer time she went bareheaded and barefooted. She was rough, coarse, ignorant, uncultivated. She helped her husband to build their log hut, to plant his grain, and to gather his crops. If Indians appeared in her husband's absence, she grasped the rifle, gathered her children about her, and with a

[1] See the monograph by Augustus H. Van Buren in the *Proceedings of the New York Historical Society*, vol. XI, p. 133.

dauntless courage defended them even unto death. This may not be a romantic presentation of the forefathers and foremothers of the State, but it bears the marks of truth and shows us a stalwart race strong to hold their own in the struggle for existence and in the establishment of a permanent community.

From the time of the founding of settlements, outward-bound ships from the Netherlands brought supplies for the colonists and carried back cargoes of furs, tobacco, and maize. In April, 1625, there was shipped to the new settlements a valuable load made up of one hundred and three head of live stock — stallions, mares, bulls, and cows — besides hogs and sheep, all distributed in two ships with a third vessel as convoy. The chronicler, Nicholaes Janszoon Van Wassenaer, gives a detailed account of their disposal which illustrates the traditional Dutch orderliness and cleanliness. He tells us that each animal had its own stall, and that the floor of each stall was covered with three feet of sand, which served as ballast for the ship. Each animal also had its respective servant, who knew what his reward was to be if he delivered his charge alive. Beneath the cattle-deck were stowed three hundred tuns of fresh water, which was pumped up for the live stock. In addition to the load of cattle, the ship carried agricultural implements and "all furniture proper for the dairy," as well as a number of settlers.

The year 1625 marked an important event, the birth of a little daughter in the household of Jan Joris Rapaelje, the "first-born Christian daughter in New Netherland." Her advent was followed by the appearance of a steadily increasing group of native citizens, and Dutch cradles multiplied in the cabins of the various settlements from Fort Orange to New Amsterdam. The latter place was established as a fortified post and the seat of government for the colony in 1626 by Peter Minuit, the third Director-General, who in this year purchased Manhattan Island from the Indians.

The colony was now thriving, with the whole settlement "bravely advanced" and grain growing as high as a man. But across this bright picture fell the dark shadow of negro slavery, which, it is said, the Dutch were the first to introduce upon the mainland north of Virginia in 1625 or 1626. Among the first slaves were Simon Congo, Anthony Portuguese, John Francisco, Paul d'Angola—

names evidently drawn from their native countries — and seven others. Two years later came
three slave women. In a letter dated August
11, 1628, and addressed to his "Kind Friend and
Well Beloved Brother in Christ the Reverend,
learned and pious Mr. Adrianus Smoutius," we
learn with regret that Domine Michaelius, having two small motherless daughters, finds himself
much hindered and distressed because he can find
no competent maid servants "and the Angola
slave women are thievish, lazy, and useless trash."

Let us leave it to those who have the heart and
the nerves to dwell upon the horrors of the middle
passage and the sufferings of the poor negroes as
set down in the log-books of the slavers, the *St.
John* and the *Arms of Amsterdam*. It is comforting
to the more soft-hearted of us to feel that after
reaching the shores of New Netherland, the blacks
were treated in the main with humanity. The
negro slave was of course a chattel, but his fate
was not without hope. Several negroes with their
wives were manumitted on the ground of long
and faithful service. They received a grant of
land; but they were obliged to pay for it annually
twenty-two and a half bushels of corn, wheat,
pease, or beans, and a hog worth eight dollars in

modern currency. If they failed in this payment they lost their recently acquired liberty and returned to the status of slaves. Meanwhile, their children, already born or yet to be born, remained under obligation to serve the Company.

Apparently the Dutch were conscious of no sense of wrong-doing in the importation of the blacks. A chief justice of the King's Bench in England expressed the opinion that it was right that pagans should be slaves to Christians, because the former were bondsmen of Satan while the latter were servants of God. Even this casuist, however, found difficulty in explaining why it was just that one born of free and Christian parents should remain enslaved. But granting that the problems which the settlers were creating in these early days were bound to cause much trouble later both to themselves and to the whole country, there is no doubt that slave labor contributed to the advancement of agriculture and the other enterprises of the colony. Free labor was scarce and expensive, owing both to the cost of importing it from Europe and to the allurements of the fur trade, which drew off the *boer-knecht* from farming. Slave labor was therefore of the highest value in exploiting the resources of the new country.

These resources were indeed abundant. The climate was temperate, with a long season of crops and harvests. Grape-vines produced an abundant supply of wines. The forests contained a vast variety of animals. Innumerable birds made the wilderness vocal. Turkeys and wild fowl offered a variety of food. The rivers produced fish of every kind and oysters which the letters of the colonists describe as a foot long, though this is somewhat staggering to the credulity of a later age. De Vries, one of the patroons, or proprietors, whose imagination was certainly of a lively type, tells us that he had seen a New Netherlander kill eighty-four thrushes or maize-birds at one shot. He adds that he has noticed crabs of excellent flavor on the flat shores of the bay. "Their claws," he says naïvely, "are of the color of our Prince's flag, orange, white and blue, so that the crabs show clearly enough that we ought to people the country and that it belongs to us." When the very crabs thus beckoned to empire, how could the Netherlanders fail to respond to their invitation?

The newly discovered river soon began to be alive with sail, high-pooped vessels from over sea, and smaller *vlie booten* (Anglicized into "flyboats"),

which plied between New Amsterdam and Fort
Orange, loaded with supplies and household goods.
Tying the prow of his boat to a tree at the water's
edge, the enterprising skipper turned pedler and
opened his packs of beguiling wares for the house-
wife at the farm beside the river. Together with
the goods in his pack, he doubtless also opened his
budget of news from the other settlements and
told the farmer's wife how the houses about the
fort at Manhattan had increased to thirty, how
the new Director was strengthening the fort,
and how all promised well for the future of New
Netherland.

For the understanding of these folk, who, with
their descendants, have left an indelible impression
on New York as we know it today, we must leave
the thread of narrative in America, abandon the
sequence of dates, and turn back to the Holland
of some years earlier. Remembering that those
who cross the sea change their skies but not their
hearts, we may be sure that the same qualities
which marked the inhabitants of the Netherlands
showed themselves in the emigrants to the colony
on the banks of the Mauritius.

When the truce with Spain was announced, a
few months before Hudson set sail for America,

it was celebrated throughout Holland by the ringing of bells, the discharge of artillery, the illumination of the houses, and the singing of hymns of thanksgiving in all the churches. The devout people knelt in every cathedral and village *Kerk* to thank their God that the period of butchery and persecution was over. But no sooner had the joybells ceased ringing and the illuminations faded than the King of Spain began plotting to regain by diplomacy what he had been unable to hold by force. The Dutch, however, showed themselves as keenly alive as the Spanish to the value of treaties and alliances. They met cunning with caution, as they had met tyranny with defiance, and at last, as the end of the truce drew near, they flung into the impending conflict the weight of the Dutch West India Company. They were shrewd and sincere people, ready to try all things by the test of practical experience. One of their great statesmen at this period described his fellow-countrymen as having neither the wish nor the skill to deceive others, but on the other hand as not being easy to be deceived themselves.

Motley says of the Dutch Republic that "it had courage, enterprise, intelligence, faith in itself, the instinct of self-government and self-help, hatred of tyranny, the disposition to domineer, aggressiveness, greediness, inquisitiveness, insolence, the love of science, of liberty, and of money." As the state is only a sum of component parts, its qualities must be those of its citizens, and of these citizens our colonists were undoubtedly typical. We may therefore accept this description as picturing their mental and spiritual qualities in the pioneer days of their venture in the New World.

CHAPTER III

PATROONS AND LORDS OF THE MANOR

THEIR High Mightinesses, the States-General of the United Netherlands, as we have seen, granted to the Dutch West India Company a charter conveying powers nearly equaling and often overlapping those of the States themselves. The West India Company in turn, with a view to stimulating colonization, granted to certain members known as patroons manorial rights frequently in conflict with the authority of the Company. And for a time it seemed as though the patroonship would be the prevailing form of grant in New Netherland.

The system of patroonships seems to have been suggested by Kiliaen Van Rensselaer, one of the directors of the West India Company and a lapidary of Amsterdam, who later became the most successful of the patroons. A shrewd, keen, far-seeing man, he was one of the first of the West India Company to perceive that the building up of

New Netherland could not be carried on without labor, and that labor could not be procured without permanent settlers. "Open up the country with agriculture: that must be our first step," was his urgent advice; but the dwellers in the Netherlands, finding themselves prosperous in their old homes, saw no reason for emigrating, and few offered themselves for the overseas settlements. The West India Company was not inclined to involve itself in further expense for colonization, and matters threatened to come to a halt, when some-one, very likely the shrewd Kiliaen himself, evolved the plan of granting large estates to men willing to pay the cost of settling and operating them. From this suggestion the scheme of patroonship was developed.

The list of "Privileges and Exemptions" published by the West India Company in 1629 declared that all should be acknowledged patroons of New Netherland who should, within the space of four years, plant there a colony of fifty souls upwards of fifteen years old. "The island of the Manhattes" was reserved for the Company. The patroons, it was stipulated, must make known the situation of their proposed settlements, but they were allowed to change should their first location prove unsatisfactory. The lands were to extend sixteen miles along the shore on one side of a navigable river, or eight miles on both sides of a river, and so far into the country as the situation of the colonies and their settlers permitted. The patroons were entitled to dispose of their grants by will, and they were free to traffic along the coast of New Netherland for all goods except furs, which were to be the special perquisite of the West India Company. They were forbidden to allow the weaving of linen, woolen, or cotton cloth on their estates, the looms in Holland being hungry for raw material.

The Company agreed that it would not take any one from the service of the patroon during the years for which the servant was bound, and any colonist who should without written permission enter the service of another patroon or "betake himself to freedom" was to be proceeded against with all the available force of the law. The escaped servant would fare ill if his case came before the courts, since it was one of the prerogatives of a patroon to administer high, middle, and low justice — that is, to appoint magistrates and erect courts which should deal with all grades of crimes committed within the limits of the manor and also with breaches of the civil law. In civil cases, disputes over contracts, titles, and such matters, where the amount in litigation exceeded twenty dollars, as well as in criminal cases affecting life and limb, it was possible to appeal to the Director and Council at Fort Amsterdam; but the local authorities craftily evaded this provision by compelling their colonists to promise not to appeal from the tribunal of the manor.

The *scherprechter*, or hangman, was included with the *superintendent*, the *schout fiscaal*, or sheriff, and the magistrates as part of the manorial court system. One such *scherprechter* named Jan de Neger, perhaps a freed negro, is named among the dwellers at Rensselaerswyck and we find him presenting a claim for thirty-eight florins ($15.00) for executing Wolf Nysen.

No man in the manorial colony was to be deprived of life or property except by sentence of a court composed of five people, and all accused persons were entitled to a speedy and impartial trial. As we find little complaint of the administration of justice in all the records of disputes, reproaches, and recriminations which mark the records of those old manors, we must assume that the processes of law were carried on in harmony with the spirit of fairness prevailing in the home country.

Even before the West India Company had promulgated its charter, a number of rich merchants had availed themselves of the opportunity to secure lands under the offered privileges and exemptions. Godyn and Blommaert, in association with Captain David de Vries and others, took up a large territory on Delaware Bay, and here they established a colony called "Swannendael," which was destroyed by the Indians in 1632. Myndert Myndertsen established his settlement on the mainland behind Staten Island, and his manor extended from Achter Kul, or Newark Bay, to the Tappan Zee.

One of the first patents recorded was granted to Michiel Pauw in 1630. In the documentary record the Director and Council of New Netherland, under the authority of their High Mightinesses, the Lords States-General and the West India Company Department of Amsterdam, testify to the bargain made with the natives, who are treated throughout with legal ceremony as if they were high contracting parties and fully capable of understanding the transaction in which they were engaged. These original owners of the soil appeared before the Council and declared that in consideration of certain merchandise, they agreed to "transfer, cede, convey and deliver for the benefit of the Honorable Mr. Michiel Paauw" as true and lawful freehold, the land at Hobocan Hackingh, opposite Manhattan, so that "he or his heirs may take possession of the aforesaid land, live on it in peace, inhabit, own and use it . . . without that they, the conveying party shall have or retain the least pretension, right, power or authority either concerning ownership or sovereignty; but herewith they desist, abandon, withdraw and renounce in behalf of aforesaid now and forever totally and finally."

It must have been a pathetic and yet a diverting spectacle when the simple red men thus swore away their title to the broad acres of their fathers for a consideration of beads, shells, blankets, and trinkets; but, when they listened to the subtleties of Dutch law as expounded by the Dogberrys at Fort Amsterdam, they may have been persuaded that their simple minds could never contend with such masters of language and that they were on the whole fortunate to secure something in exchange for their land, which they were bound to lose in any event.

It has been the custom to ascribe to the Dutch and Quakers the system of paying for lands taken from the Indians. But Fiske points out that this conception is a mistake and he goes on to state that it was a general custom among the English and that not a rood of ground in New England was taken from the savages without recompense, except when the Pequots began a war and were exterminated. The "payment" in all cases, however, was a mere farce and of value only in creating good feeling between savages and settlers. As to the ethics of the transaction, much might be said on both sides. The red men would be justified in feeling that they had been kept in ignorance of the relative importance of what they gave and what they received, while the whites might maintain that they created the values which ensued upon their purchase and that, if they had not come, lands along the Great River would have remained of little account. In any case the recorded transaction did not prove a financial triumph for the purchaser, as the enterprise cost much in trouble and outlay and did not meet expenses. The property was resold to the Company seven years later — at a price, however, of twenty-six thousand guilders, which represented a fair margin of profit over the "certain merchandise" paid to the original owners eight years earlier.

Very soon after the purchase of the land on the west shore of the North River, Pauw bought, under the same elaborate legal forms, the whole of Staten Island, so called in honor of the *Staaten* or States-General. To the estate he gave the title of Pavonia, a Latinized form of his own name. Staten Island was subsequently purchased from Pauw by the Company and transferred (with the exception of the *bouwerie* of Captain De Vries) to Cornelis Melyn, who was thus added to the list of patroons. Other regions also were erected into patroonships; but almost all were either unsuccessful from the beginning or short-lived.

The patroonship most successful, most permanent, and most typical was Rensselaerswyck, which offers the best opportunity for a study of the Dutch colonial system. Van Rensselaer, though he did not apparently intend to make a home for himself in New Netherland, was one of the first to ask for a grant of land. He received, subject to payment to the Indians, a tract of country to the north and south of Fort Orange, but not including that trading-post, which like the island of Manhattan remained under the control of the West India Company. By virtue of this grant and later purchases Van Rensselaer acquired a

tract comprising what are now the counties of
Albany and Rensselaer with part of Columbia.
Of this tract, called Rensselaerswyck, Van Rensselaer was named patroon, and five other men,
Godyn, Blommaert, De Laet, Bissels, and Mous-
sart, whom he had been forced to conciliate by
taking into partnership, were named codirectors.
Later the claims of these five associates were
bought out by the Van Rensselaer family.

In 1630 the first group of emigrants for this new
colony sailed on the ship *Eendragt* and reached
Fort Orange at the beginning of June. How crude
was the settlement which they established we may
judge from the report made some years later by
Father Jogues, a Jesuit missionary, who visited
Rensselaerswyck in 1643. He speaks of a miser-
able little fort built of logs and having four or five
pieces of Breteuil cannon. He describes also the
colony as composed of about a hundred persons,
"who reside in some twenty-five or thirty houses
built along the river as each found most convenient." The patroon's agent was established in
the principal house, while in another, which served
also as a church, was domiciled the *domine*, the
Reverend Johannes Megapolensis, Jr. The houses
he describes as built of boards and roofed with

thatch, having no mason-work except in the chimneys. The settlers had found some ground already cleared by the natives and had planted it with wheat and oats in order to provide beer and horse-fodder; but being hemmed in by somewhat barren hills, they had been obliged to separate in order to obtain arable land. The settlements, therefore, spread over two or three leagues.

The fear of raids from the savages prompted the patroon to advise that, with the exception of the brewers and tobacco planters who were obliged to live on their plantations, no other settlers should establish themselves at any distance from the church, which was the village center; for, says the prudent Van Rensselaer, "every one residing where he thinks fit, separated far from others, would be unfortunately in danger of their lives in the same manner as sorrowful experience has taught around the Manhattans." Our sympathy goes out to those early settlers who lived almost as serfs under their patroon, the women forbidden to spin or weave, the men prohibited from trading in the furs which they saw building up fortunes around them. They sat by their lonely hearths in a little clearing of the forest, listening to the howl of wolves and fearing to see a savage face at the window. This existence was a tragic change indeed from the lively social existence along the canals of Amsterdam or on the stoops of Rotter-dam.

Nor can we feel that these tenants were likely to be greatly cheered by the library established at Rensselaerswyck, unless there were hidden away a list of more interesting books than those described in the patroon's invoice as sent in an *oosterse*, or oriental, box. These volumes include a Scripture concordance, the works of Calvin, of Livy, and of Ursinus, the friend of Melanchthon, *A Treatise on Arithmetic* by Adrian Metius, *The History of the Holy Land*, and a work on natural theology. As all the titles are in Latin, it is to be presumed that the body of the text was written in the same language, and we may imagine the light and cheerful mood which they inspired in their readers after a day of manual toil.

I suspect, however, that the evening hours of these tenants at Rensselaerswyck were spent in anxious keeping of accounts with a wholesome fear of the patroon before the eyes of the accountants. Life on the *bouweries* was by no means inexpensive, even according to modern standards. Bearing in mind that a stiver was equivalent to two cents of

our currency and a florin to forty cents, it is easy
to calculate the cost of living in the decade between 1630 and 1640 as set down in the accounts
of Rensselaerswyck. A blanket cost eight florins,
a hat ten florins, an iron anvil one hundred florins,
a musket and cartouche box nineteen florins, a
copper sheep's bell one florin and six stivers. On
the other hand all domestic produce was cheap,
because the tenant and patroon preferred to dispose of it in the settlements rather than by trans-
porting it to New Amsterdam. We learn with
envy that butter was only eight stivers or sixteen
cents per pound, a pair of fowl two florins, a beaver
twenty-five florins.

How hard were the terms on which the tenants
held their leases is apparent from a report written
by the guardians and tutors of Jan Van Rensselaer, a later patroon of Rensselaerswyck. The
patroon reserved to himself the tenth of all grains,
fruits, and other products raised on the *bouwerie*.
The tenant was bound, in addition to his rent of
five hundred guilders or two hundred dollars, to
keep up the roads, repair the buildings, cut ten
pieces of oak or fir wood, and bring the same to the
shore; he must also every year give to the patroon
three day' service with his horses and wagon;

each year he was to cut, split, and bring to the waterside two fathoms of firewood; and he was further to deliver yearly to the Director as quit-rent two bushels of wheat, twenty-five pounds of butter, and two pairs of fowls.

It was the difficult task of the agent of the colony to harmonize the constant hostilities between the patroon and his "people." Van Curler's letter to Kiliaen Van Rensselaer begins: "Laus Deo! At the Manhattans this 16th June, 1643, Most honorable, wise, powerful, and right discreet Lord, my Lord Patroon —." After which propitiatory beginning it embarks at once on a reply to the reproaches which the honorable, wise, and powerful Lord has heaped upon his obedient servant. Van Curler admits that the accounts and books have not been forwarded to Holland as they should have been; but he pleads the difficulty of securing returns from the tenants, whom he finds slippery in their accounting. "Everything they have laid out on account of the Lord Patroon they well know how to specify for what was expended. But what has been laid out for their private use, that they know nothing about."

If the patroon's relations with his tenants were thorny, he had no less trouble in his dealings with the Director-General at New Amsterdam. It is true, Peter Minuit, the first important Director, was removed in 1632 by the Company for unduly favoring the patroons, and Van Twiller, another Director and a nephew of Van Rensselaer by marriage, was not disposed to antagonize his relative; but when Van Twiller was replaced by Kieft, and he in turn by Stuyvesant, the horizon at Rensselaerswyck grew stormy. In 1643 the patroon ordered Nicholas Coorn to fortify Beeren or Bears Island, and to demand a toll of each ship, except those of the West India Company, that passed up and down the river. He also required that the colors on every ship be lowered in passing Rensselaer's Stein or Castle Rensselaer, as the fort on the steep little island was named.

Govert Loockermans, sailing down the river one day on the ship *Good Hope*, failed to salute the flag, whereupon a lively dialogue ensued to the following effect, and not, we may be assured, carried on in low or amicable tones:

Coorn: "Lower your colors!"

Loockermans: "For whom should I?"

Coorn: "For the staple-right of Rensselaerswyck."

Loockermans: "I lower my colors for no one

except the Prince of Orange and the Lords my masters."

The practical result of this interchange of amenities was a shot which tore the mainsail of the *Good Hope*, "perforated the princely flag," and so enraged the skipper that on his arrival at New Amsterdam he hastened to lay his grievance before the Council, who thereupon ordered Coorn to behave with more civility.

The patroon system was from the beginning doomed to failure. As we study the old documents we find a sullen tenantry, an obsequious and careworn agent, a dissatisfied patroon, an impatient company, a bewildered government — and all this in a new and promising country where the natives were friendly, the transportation easy, the land fertile, the conditions favorable to that conservation of human happiness which is and should be the aim of civilization. The reason for the discontent which prevailed is not far to seek, and all classes were responsible for it, for they combined in planting an anachronistic feudalism in a new country, which was dedicated by its very physical conditions to liberty and democracy. The settlers came from a nation which had battled through long years in the cause of freedom. They found themselves in a colony adjoining those of Englishmen who had braved the perils of the wilderness to establish the same principles of liberty and democracy. No sane mind could have expected the Dutch colonists to return without protest to a medieval system of government.

When the English took possession of New Netherland in 1664, the old patroonships were confirmed as manorial grants from England. As time went on, many new manors were erected until, when the province was finally added to England in 1674, "The Lords of the Manor" along the Hudson had taken on the proportions of a landed aristocracy. On the lower reaches of the river lay the Van Cortlandt and Philipse Manors, the first containing 85,000 acres and a house so firmly built that it is still standing with its walls of freestone, three feet thick. The Philipse Manor, at Tarrytown, represented the remarkable achievement of a self-made man, born in the Old World and a carpenter by trade, who rose in the New World to fortune and eminence. By dint of business acumen and by marrying two heiresses in succession he achieved wealth, and built "Castle Philipse" and the picturesque little church at Sleepy Hollow,

still in use. Farther up the river lay the Livingston Manor. In 1685 Robert Livingston was
granted by Governor Dongan a patent of a tract
half way between New York and Rensselaerswyck,
across the river from the Catskills and covering
many thousand acres.

But the estate of which we know most, thanks
to the records left by Mrs. Grant of Laggan in her
Memoirs of an American Lady, written in the
middle of the eighteenth century, is that belonging
to the Schuylers at "the Flats" near Albany,
which runs along the western bank of the Hudson
for two miles and is bordered with sweeping elm
trees. The mansion consisted of two stories and
an attic. Through the middle of the house ran
a wide passage from the front to the back door.
At the front door was a large *stoep*, open at the
sides and with seats around it. One room was
open for company. The other apartments were
bedrooms, a drawing-room being an unheard-of
luxury. "The house fronted the river, on the
brink of which, under shades of elm and sycamore,
ran the great road toward Saratoga, Stillwater,
and the northern lakes." Adjoining the orchard
was a huge barn raised from the ground by beams
which rested on stone and held up a massive oak

floor. On one side ran a manger. Cattle and horses stood in rows with their heads toward the threshing-floor. "There was a prodigious large box or open chest in one side built up, for holding the corn after it was threshed, and the roof which was very lofty and spacious was supported by large cross beams. From one to the other of these was stretched a great number of long poles so as to form a sort of open loft, on which the whole rich crop was laid up."

Altogether it is an attractive picture of peace and plenty, of hospitality and simple luxury, that is drawn by this visitor to the Schuyler homestead. We see through her eyes its carpeted winter rooms, its hall covered with tiled oilcloth and hung with family portraits, its vine-covered *stoeps*, provided with ledges for the birds, and affording "pleasant views of the winding river and the distant hills." Such a picture relieves pleasantly the arid waste of historical statistics.

But the reader who dwells too long on the picturesque aspects of manors and patroonships is likely to forget that New Netherland was peopled for the most part by colonists who were neither patroons nor lords of manors. It was the small proprietors who eventually predominated on western

Long Island, on Staten Island, and along the
Hudson. "In the end," it has been well said,
"this form of grant played a more important part
in the development of the province than did the
larger fiefs for which such detailed provision was
made."

CHAPTER IV

THE DIRECTORS

THE first Director-General of the colony, Captain Cornelis May, was removed by only a generation from those "Beggars of the Sea" whom the Spaniard held in such contempt; but this mendicant had begged to such advantage that the sea granted him a noble river to explore and a cape at its mouth to preserve his name to posterity. It is upon his discoveries along the South River, later called the Delaware, and not upon his record as Director of New Netherland, that his title to fame must rest. Associated with him was Tienpont, who appears to have been assigned to the North River while May assumed personal supervision of the South. May acted as the agent of the West India Company for one year only (1624–1625), and was followed in office by Verhulst (1625–1626), who bequeathed his name to Verhulsten Island, in the Delaware River, and then quietly passed out of history.

Neither of these officials left any permanent impress on the history of the colony. It was therefore a day of vast importance to the dwellers on the North River, and especially to the little group of settlers on Manhattan Island, when the *Meeuwken* dropped her anchor in the harbor in May, 1626, and her small boat landed Peter Minuit, Director-General of New Netherland, a Governor who had come to govern. Minuit, though registered as "of Wesel," Germany, was of Huguenot ancestry, and is reported to have spoken French, Dutch, German, and English. He proved a tactful and efficient ruler, and the new system of government took form under the Director and Council, the *koopman*, who was commercial agent and secretary, and a *schout* who performed the duties of sheriff and public prosecutor.

Van Wassenaer, the son of a *domine* in Amsterdam, gives us a report of the colony as it existed under Minuit. He writes of a counting-house built of stone and thatched with reeds, of thirty ordinary houses on the east side of the river, and a horse-mill yet unfinished over which is to be constructed a spacious room to serve as a temporary church and to be decorated with bells captured at the sack of San Juan de Porto Rico in 1625 by the Dutch fleet.

shipbuilding project of great magnitude for tha
time. Two Belgian shipbuilders arrived in New
Amsterdam and asked the help of the Director
in constructing a large vessel. Minuit, seeing
the opportunity to advertise the resources of the
colony, agreed to give his assistance and the result
was that the *New Netherland*, a ship of eight hundred tons carrying thirty guns, was built and
launched.

This enterprise cost more than had been expected and the bills were severely criticized by the
West India Company, already dissatisfied with
Minuit on the ground that he had favored the
interests of the patroons, who claimed the right of
unrestricted trade within their estates, as against
the interests of the Company. Urged by many
complaints, the States-General set on foot an in-
vestigation of the Director, the patroons, and the
West India Company itself, with the result that in
32 Minuit was recalled and the power of the
patroons was limited. New Netherland had not
seen the last of Peter Minuit, however. Angry
and embittered, he entered the service of Sweden
and returned later to vex the Dutch colony.

In the interval between Minuit's departure and
the arrival of Van Twiller, the reins of authority

According to this chronicler, every one in New
Netherland who fills no public office is busy with
his own affairs. One trades, one builds houses,
another plants farms. Each farmer pastures the
cows under his charge on the *bouwerie* of the Company, which also owns the cattle; but the milk is
the property of the farmer, who sells it to the
settlers. "The houses of settlers," he says, "are
now outside the fort; but when that is finished
they will all remove within, in order to garrison it
and be safe from sudden attack."

One of Minuit's first acts as Director was the
purchase of Manhattan Island, covering some
twenty-two thousand acres, for merchandise
valued at sixty guilders or twenty-four dollars.
He thus secured the land at the rate of approximately ten acres for one cent. A good bargain,
Peter Minuit! The transaction was doubly effec-
tive in placating the savages, or the *wilden*, as the
settlers called them, and in establishing the Dutch
claim as against the English by urging rights both
of discovery and of purchase.

In spite of the goodwill manifested by the
natives, the settlers were constantly anxious lest
some conspiracy might suddenly break out. Van
Wassenaer, reporting the news from the colony as

it reached him in Amsterdam, wrote in 1626 that Pieter Barentsen was to be sent to command Fort Orange, and that the families were to be brought down the river, sixteen men without women being left to garrison the fort. Two years later he wrote that there were no families at Fort Orange, all having been brought down the river. Only twenty-five or twenty-six traders remained and Krol, who had been vice-director there since 1626.

Minuit showed true statesmanship by following conciliation with a show of strength against hostile powers on every hand. He had brought with him a competent engineer, Kryn Frederycke, or Fredericksen, who had been an officer in the army of Prince Maurice. With his help Minuit laid out Fort Amsterdam on what was then the tip of Manhattan Island, the green park which forms the end of the island today being then under water. Fredericksen found material and labor so scarce that he could plan at first only a blockhouse surrounded by palisades of red cedar strengthened with earthworks. The fort was completed in 1626, and at the close of the year a settlement called New Amsterdam had grown up around it and had been made the capital of New Netherland.

During the building of the fort there occurred

an episode fraught with serious consequence friendly Indian of the Weckquaesgeeck tribe with his nephew to traffic at Fort Amste Three servants of Minuit fell upon the I robbed him, and murdered him. The n then but a boy, escaped to his tribe and a vengeance which he wreaked in blood score of years later.

Minuit's preparations for war were not to land fortification. In 1627 the hear colonists were gladdened by a great the Dutch over the Spanish, when, in a San Salvador, Peter Heyn demolished Spanish warships. On the 5th of Sep same bold sailor captured the whole of silver-fleet with spoils amounting to tw guilders. In the following year the mander, then a lieutenant-admiral, d on the deck of his ship. The States to his old peasant mother a message to which she replied: "Ay, I thoug be the end of him. He was alway but I did my best to correct him. than he deserved."

It was perhaps the echo of na these which prompted Minuit to

were held by Sebastian Krol, whose name is memorable chiefly for the fact that he had been influential in purchasing the domain of Rensselaerswyck for its patroon (1630) and the tradition that the cruller, *crolyer* or *krolyer*, was so called in his honor. The Company's selection of a permanent successor to Minuit was not happy. Wouter Van Twiller, nephew of Kiliaen Van Rensselaer, must have owed his appointment as Director to family influence, since neither his career nor his reputation justified the choice.

David de Vries, writing on April 16, 1633, notes that on arriving about noon before Fort Amsterdam he found there a ship called the *Soutbergh* which had brought over the new Governor, Wouter Van Twiller, a former clerk in the West India House at Amsterdam. De Vries gives his opinion of Van Twiller in no uncertain terms. He expressed his own surprise that the West India Company should send fools into this country who knew nothing except how to drink, and quotes an Englishman as saying that he could not understand the unruliness among the officers of the Company and that a governor should have no more control over them.

For the personal appearance of this "Walter

the Doubter," we must turn again to the testimony of Knickerbocker, whose mocking descriptions have obtained a quasi-historical authority:

This renowned old gentleman arrived at New Amsterdam in the merry month of June. . . . He was exactly five feet six inches in height and six feet five inches in circumference. His head was a perfect sphere and of such stupendous dimensions that Dame Nature, with all her sex's ingenuity would have been puzzled to construct a neck capable of supporting it: Wherefore she wisely declined the attempt and settled it firmly on the top of his backbone just between the shoulders. . . . His legs were short but sturdy in proportion to the weight they had to sustain so that when erect he had not a little the appearance of a beer barrel on skids. His face, that infallible index of the mind, presented a vast expanse, unfurrowed by any of those lines which disfigure the human countenance with what is termed expression. . . . His habits were regular. He daily took his four stated meals, appropriating exactly an hour to each; he smoked and doubted eight hours, and he slept the remaining twelve of the four-and-twenty.

A later historian, taking up the cudgels in behalf of the Director, resents Knickerbocker's impeachment and protests that "so far from being the aged, fat and overgrown person represented in caricature Van Twiller was youthful and inexperienced, and his faults were those of a young man unused to authority and hampered by his instructions." [1]

In his new office Van Twiller was confronted with questions dealing with the encroachment of the patroons from within and of the English from without, the unwelcome visit of Eelkens, of whom we shall hear later, and massacres by the Indians on the South River. Such problems might well have puzzled a wiser head and a more determined character than Van Twiller's. We cannot hold him wholly blameworthy if he dealt with them in a spirit of doubt and hesitation. What we find harder to excuse is his shrewd advancement of his own interests and his lavish expenditure of the Company's money. The cost of building the fort

---

[1] Van Twiller's advocate, W. E. Griffis, quotes the Nijkerk records in proof that Van Twiller was born on May 22, 1606, which would fix his age at twenty-seven when he was sent out to the colony. The editor of the Van Rensselaer-Bowier manuscript states that Kiliaen Van Rensselaer was born in 1580, that his sister, Maria, married Richard, or Ryckaert, Van Twiller and that the Wouter of our chronicles was their son and therefore Van Rensselaer's nephew. We are the more inclined to accept the year 1606 as the true date of Van Twiller's birth because the year 1580, previously accepted by historians, would have been the same as that of the birth of Kiliaen Van Rensselaer himself, and because, according to the author of the *Story of New Netherland*, Maria Van Rensselaer was betrothed in 1605. Otherwise we should find it almost beyond credence that a youth of twenty-seven should have been so suddenly promoted from the counting-house at Amsterdam to the responsible post of Director of New Netherland.

was more than justifiable. To have neglected the defenses would have been culpable; and the barracks built for the hundred and four soldiers whom he had brought over from the Fatherland may also be set down as necessary. But when the Company was groaning under the expenses of the colony, it was, to say the least, lacking in tact to build for himself the most elaborate house in New Netherland, besides erecting on one of the Company's *bouweries* a house, a barn, a boathouse, and a brewery, to say nothing of planting another farm with tobacco, working it with slave labor at the Company's expense, and appropriating the profits. In the year 1638, after he had been five years in office, the outcry against Van Twiller for misfeasance, malfeasance, and especially nonfeasance, grew too loud to be ignored, and he was recalled; but before he left New Netherland he bought Nooten or Nut Island, since called Governor's Island, and also two other islands in the East River. At the time of his marriage in 1643, Van Twiller was in command of a competence attained at the expense of the West India Company, and there is much excuse for the feeling of his employers that he had been more active in his own affairs than in theirs.

The principal service which he had rendered to the Company in his term of office was the establishment of "staple right" at New Amsterdam, compelling all ships trading on the coast or the North River to pay tolls or unload their cargoes on the Company's property. But on the reverse side of the account we must remember that he allowed the fort to fall into such decay that when Kieft arrived in 1638 he found the defenses, which had been finished only three years before, already in a shamefully neglected condition, the guns dismounted, the public buildings inside the walls in ruins, and the walls of the fort itself so beaten down that any one might enter at will, "save at the stone point."

The hopes of the colonists rose again with the coming of a new governor; but the appointment of Kieft reflected as little credit as that of Van Twiller upon the sagacity of the West India Company. The man now chosen to rule New Netherland was a narrow-minded busybody, eager to interfere in small matters and without the statesmanship required to conduct large affairs. Some of his activities, it is true, had practical value. He fixed the hours at which the colonists should go to bed and ordered the curfew to be rung at nine o'clock;

he established two annual fairs to be held on the present Bowling Green, one in October for cattle and one in November for hogs; and he built a new stone church within the fort, operated a brewery, founded a hostelry, and planted orchards and gardens. But on the other side of the account he was responsible for a bloody war with the Indians which came near to wrecking the colony.

His previous record held scant promise for his success as a governor. He had failed as a merchant in Rochelle, for which offense his portrait had been affixed to a gallows. Such a man was a poor person to be put in control of the complicated finances of New Netherland and of the delicate relations between the colonists and the Indians — relations calling for infinite tact, wisdom, firmness, and forbearance.

The natives in the region of New Amsterdam were increasingly irritated by the encroachments of the whites. They complained that stray cows spoiled their unfenced cornfields and that various other depredations endangered their crops. To add to this irritation Kieft proposed to tax the natives for the protection afforded them by the Fort, which was now being repaired at large expense. The situation, already bad enough, was further complicated by Kieft's clumsy handling of an altercation on Staten Island. Some pigs were stolen, by servants of the Company as appeared later; but the offense was charged to the Raritan Indians. Without waiting to make investigations Kieft sent out a punitive expedition of seventy men, who attacked the innocent natives, killed a number of them, and laid waste their crops. This stupid and wicked attack still further exasperated the Indians, who in the high tide of midsummer saw their lands laid bare and their homes desolated by the wanton hand of the intruders.

Some months later the trouble between the whites and the red men was brought to a head by an unforeseen tragedy. A savage came to Claes Smits, *radenmaker* or wheelwright, to trade beaver for duffel cloth. As Claes stooped down to take out the duffel from a chest, the Indian seized an axe which chanced to stand near by and struck the wheelwright on the neck, killing him instantly. The murderer then stole the goods from the chest and fled to the forest.

When Kieft sent to the tribe of the Weckquaesgeecks to inquire the cause of this murder and to demand the slayer, the Indian told the chief that he had seen his uncle robbed and killed at the fort while it was being built; that he himself had escaped and had vowed revenge; and that the unlucky Claes was the first white man upon whom he had a chance to wreak vengeance. The chief then replied to the Director that he was sorry that twenty Christians had not been killed and that the Indian had done only a pious duty in avenging his uncle.

In this emergency Kieft called a meeting at which the prominent burghers chose a committee of twelve to advise the Director. This took place in 1641. The Council was headed by Captain David de Vries, whose portrait with its pointed chin, high forehead, and keen eyes, justifies his reputation as the ablest man in New Netherland. He insisted that it was inadvisable to attack the Indians — not to say hazardous. Besides, the Company had warned them to keep peace. It is interesting to speculate on what would have been the effect on the colony if the Company's choice had fallen upon De Vries instead of on Kieft as Director.

Although restrained for the time, Kieft never relinquished his purpose. On February 24, 1643, he again announced his intention of making a raid upon the Indians, and in spite of further remon-

strance from De Vries he sent out his soldiers, who
returned after a massacre which disgraced the
Director, enraged the natives, and endangered the
colony. Kieft was at first proud of his treachery;
but as soon as it was known every Algonquin tribe
around New Amsterdam started on the warpath.
From New Jersey to the Connecticut every farm
was in peril. The famous and much-persecuted
Anne Hutchinson perished with her family; towns
were burned; and men, women, and children fled
in panic.

On the approach of spring, when the Indians had
to plant their corn or face famine, sachems of the
Long Island Indians sought a parley with the
Dutch. De Vries and Olfertsen volunteered to
meet the savages. In the woods near Rockaway
they found nearly three hundred Indians assembled. The chiefs placed the envoys in the
center of the circle, and one among them, who had
a bundle of sticks, laid down one stick at a time as
he recounted the wrongs of his tribe. This orator
told how the red men had given food to the settlers
and were rewarded by the murder of their people,
how they had protected and cherished the traders,
and how they had been abused in return. At
length De Vries, like the practical man that he was,

suggested that they all adjourn to the Fort, promising them presents from the Director.

The chiefs consented to meet the Director and eventually were persuaded to make a treaty of peace; but Kieft's gifts were so niggardly that the savages went away with rancor still in their hearts, and the war of the races continued its bloody course. It is no wonder that when De Vries left the Governor on this occasion, he told Kieft in plain terms of his guilt and predicted that the shedding of so much innocent blood would yet be avenged upon his own head. This prophecy proved a strangely true one. When recalled by the States-General in 1647, Kieft set out for Holland on the ship *Princess*, carrying with him the sum of four hundred thousand guilders. The ship was wrecked in the Bristol channel and Kieft was drowned.

The evil that Kieft did lived after him and the good, if interred with his bones, would not have occupied much space in the tomb. The only positive advance during his rule — and that was carried through against his will — was the appointment of an advisory committee of the twelve men, representing the householders of the colony, who were called together in the emergency following the murder of Claes Smits, and in 1643 of a similar board of eight men, who protested against his arbitrary measures and later procured his recall.

After the departure of Kieft the most picturesque figure of the period of Dutch rule in America appeared at New Amsterdam, Petrus or Pieter Stuyvesant. We have an authentic portrait in which the whole personality of the man is writ large. The dominant nose, the small, obstinate eyes, the close-set, autocratic mouth, tell the character of the man who was come to be the new and the last Director-General of New Netherland. As Director of the West India Company's colony at Curaçao, Stuyvesant had undertaken the task of reducing the Portuguese island of St. Martin and had lost a leg in the fight. This loss he repaired with a wooden leg, of which he professed himself prouder than of all his other limbs together and which he had decorated with silver bands and nails, thus earning for him the sobriquet of "Old Silver Nails." Still, so the legend runs, Peter Stuyvesant's ghost at night "stumps to and fro with a shadowy wooden leg through the aisles of St. Mark's Church near the spot where his bones lie buried." But many events were to happen before those bones were laid in the family vault of the chapel on his *bouwerie*.

When Stuyvesant reached the country over which he was to rule, it was noted by the colonists that his bearing was that of a prince. "I shall be as a father over his children," he told the burghers of New Amsterdam, and in this patriarchal capacity he kept the people standing with their heads uncovered for more than an hour, while he wore his hat. How he bore out this first impression we may gather from *The Representation of New Netherland*, an arraignment of the Director, drawn up and solemnly attested in 1650 by eleven responsible burghers headed by Adrian Van der Donck, and supplemented by much detailed evidence. The witnesses express the earnest wish that Stuyvesant's administration were at an end, for they have suffered from it and know themselves powerless. Whoever opposes the Director "hath as much as the sun and moon against him." In the council he writes an opinion covering several pages and then adds orally: "This is my opinion. If anyone have aught to object to it, let him express it!" If any one ventures to make any objection, his Honor flies into a passion and rails in language better fitted to the fish-market than to the council-hall.

When two burghers, Kuyter and Melyn, who had been leaders of the opposition to Kieft, petitioned Stuyvesant to investigate his conduct, Stuyvesant supported his predecessor on the ground that one Director should uphold another. At Kieft's instigation he even prosecuted and convicted Kuyter and Melyn for seditious attack on the government. When Melyn asked for grace till his case could be presented in the Fatherland, he was threatened, according to his own testimony, in language like this: "If I knew, Melyn, that you would divulge our sentence [that of fine and banishment] or bring it before Their High Mightinesses, I would cause you to be hanged at once on the highest tree in New Netherland." In another case the Director said: "It may during my administration be contemplated to appeal; but if anyone should do it, I will make him a foot shorter, and send the pieces to Holland and let him appeal in that way."

An answer to this arraignment by the burghers of New Netherland was written by Van Tienhoven, who was sent over to the Netherlands to defend Stuyvesant; but its value is impaired by the fact that he was *schout fiscaal* and interested in the acquittal of Stuyvesant, whose tool he was, and also by the fact that he was the subject of bitter attack in the *Representation* by Adrian Van der Donck, who accused Van Tienhoven of continually shifting from one side to another and asserted that he was notoriously profligate and untrustworthy. One passage in his reply amounted to a confession. Who, he asks, are they who have complained about the haughtiness of the Director, and he answers that they are "such as seek to live without law or rule." "No one," he goes on to say, "can prove that Director Stuyvesant has used foul language to or railed at as clowns any respectable persons who have treated him decently. It may be that some profligate person has given the Director, *if he has used any bad words to him*, cause to do so."

It has been the fashion in popular histories to allude to Stuyvesant as a doughty knight of somewhat choleric temper, "a valiant, weather beaten, leathern-sided, lion-hearted, generous-spirited, old governor"; but I do not so read his history. I find him a brutal tyrant, as we have seen in the affair of Kieft *versus* Melyn; a narrow-minded bigot, as we shall see later in his dealing with the Quakers at Flushing; a bully when his victims were completely in his power; and a loser in any quarrel when he was met with blustering comparable to his own.

In support of the last indictment let us take his conduct in a conflict with the authorities at Rensselaerswyck. In 1646 Stuyvesant had ordered that no building should be erected within cannon-shot of Fort Orange. The superintendent of the settlement denied Stuyvesant's right to give such an order and pointed to the fact that his trading-house had been for a long time on the border of the fort. To the claim that a clear space was necessary to the fort's efficiency, Van Slichtenhorst, Van Rensselaer's agent, replied that he had spent more than six months in the colony and had never seen a single person carrying a sword, musket, or pike, nor had he heard a drum-beat except on the occasion of a visit from the Director and his soldiers in the summer. Stuyvesant rejoined by sending soldiers and sailors to tear down the house which Van Slichtenhorst was building near Fort Orange, and the commissary was ordered to arrest the builder if he resisted; but the commissary wrote that it would be impossible to carry out the order, as the settlers at Rensselaerswyck, reënforced by the Indians, outnumbered his troops. Stuyvesant then recalled his soldiers and ordered Van

Slichtenhorst to appear before him, which the agent refused to do.

In 1652 Stuyvesant ordered Dyckman, then in command at Fort Orange, not to allow any one to build a house near the fort or to remain in any house already built. In spite of proclamations and other bluster this order proved fruitless and on April 1, 1653, Stuyvesant came in person to Fort Orange and sent a sergeant to lower the patroon's flag. The agent refusing to strike the patroon's colors, the soldiers entered, lowered the flag, and discharged their guns. Stuyvesant declared that the region staked out by posts should be known as Beverwyck and instituted a court there. Van Slichtenhorst tore down the proclamation, whereupon Stuyvesant ordered him to be imprisoned in the fort. Later the Director transported the agent under guard to New Amsterdam.

Stuyvesant's arbitrary character also appears in his overriding of the measure of local self-government decreed by the States-General in 1653. Van der Donck and his fellows had asked three things of their High Mightinesses, the States-General: first, that they take over the government of New Netherland; second, that they establish a better city government in New Amsterdam; and third, that they clearly define the boundaries of New Netherland. The first of these requests, owing to the deeply intrenched interest of the West India Company, could not be granted, the last still less. But the States-General urged that municipal rights should be given to New Amsterdam, and in 1652 the Company yielded. The charter limited the number of *schepens* or aldermen to five and the number of burgomasters to two, and also ordained that they as well as the *schout* should be elected by the citizens; but Stuyvesant ignored this provision and proceeded to appoint men of his own choosing. The Stone Tavern built by Kieft at the head of Coenties Slip was set apart as a *Stadt-Huys*, or City Hall, and here Stuyvesant's appointees, supposed to represent the popular will, held their meetings. It was something that they did hold meetings and nominally at least in the interest of the people. Another concession followed. In 1658 Stuyvesant yielded so far to the principles of popular government as to concede to the *schepens* and burgomasters of New Amsterdam the right to nominate double the number of candidates for office, from whom the Director was to make a choice.

In 1655, during the absence of Stuyvesant on the South River, the Indians around Manhattan appeared with a fleet of sixty-four war canoes, attacked and looted New Amsterdam, then crossed to Hoboken and continued their bloody work in Pavonia and on Staten Island. In three days a hundred men, women, and children were slain, and a hundred and fifty-two were taken captive, and the damage to property was estimated at two hundred thousand guilders — approximately eighty thousand dollars. As usual the Dutch had been the aggressors, for Van Dyck, formerly *schout fiscaal*, had shot and killed an old Indian woman who was picking peaches in his orchard.

It must be set down to Stuyvesant's credit that on his return he acted toward the Indians in a manner that was kind and conciliating, and at the same time provided against a repetition of the recent disaster by erecting blockhouses at various points and by concentrating the settlers for mutual defense. By this policy of mingled diplomacy and preparation against attack Stuyvesant preserved peace for a period of three years. But trouble with the Indians continued to disturb the colonies on the river and centered at Esopus, where slaughters of both white and red men occurred. Eight white men were burned at the stake in revenge for shots fired by Dutch soldiers, and an Indian chief was killed with his own tomahawk. In 1660 a treaty of peace was framed; but three years later we find the two races again embroiled. Thus Indian wars continued down to the close of Dutch rule.

In spite of these troubles in the more outlying districts, New Amsterdam continued to grow and thrive. In Stuyvesant's time the thoroughfares of New Amsterdam were laid out as streets and were named. The line of houses facing the fort on the eastern side was called the Marckveldt, or Marketfield, taking its name from the green opposite, which had been the site of the city market. De Heere Straat, the principal street, ran north from the fort through the gate at the city wall. De Hoogh Straat ran parallel with the East River from the city bridge to the water gate and on its line stood the *Stadt-Huys*. 'T Water ran in a semi-circular line from the point of the island and was bordered by the East River. De Brouwer Straat took its name from the breweries situated on it and was probably the first street in the town to be regulated and paved. De Brugh Straat, as the name implies, led to the bridge crossing. De Heere Graft, the principal canal, was a creek running deep into the island from the East River and protected by a siding of boards. An official was appointed for the care of this canal with orders to see "that the newly made *graft* was kept in order, that no filth was cast into it, and that the boats, canoes, and other vessels were laid in order."

The new city was by this time thoroughly cosmopolitan. One traveler speaks of the use of eighteen different languages, and the forms of faith were as varied as the tongues spoken. Seven or eight large ships came every year from Amsterdam. The Director occupied a fine house on the point of the island. On the east side of the town stood the *Stadt-Huys* protected by a half-moon of stone mounted with three small brass cannon. In the fort stood the Governor's house, the church, the barracks, the house for munitions, and the long-armed windmills. Everything was prospering except the foundation on which all depended. There was no adequate defense for all this property. Here we must acquit Stuyvesant from responsibility, since again and again he had warned the Company against the weakness of the colony; but they would not heed the warnings, and the consequences which might have been averted suddenly overtook the Dutch possessions.

The war which broke out in 1652 between

England and the Netherlands, once leagued against
Catholic Spain but now parted by commercial
rivalries, found an immediate echo on the shores
of the Hudson. With feverish haste the inhabitants of New Amsterdam began to fortify. Across
the island at the northern limit of the town, on the
line of what is now Wall Street, they built a wall
with stout palisades backed by earthworks. They
hastily repaired the fort, organized the citizens as
far as possible to resist attack, and also strengthened Fort Orange. The New England Colonies
likewise began warlike preparations; but, perhaps
owing to the prudence of Stuyvesant in accepting
the Treaty of Hartford, peace between the Dutch
and English in the New World continued for the
present, though on precarious terms; and, the immediate threat of danger being removed by the
treaty between England and Holland in 1654, the
New Netherlanders relaxed their vigilance and
curtailed the expense of fortifications.

Meanwhile Stuyvesant had alienated popular
sympathy and lessened united support by his
treatment of a convention of delegates from New
Amsterdam, Flushing, Breuckelen, Hempstead,
Amersfort, Middleburgh, Flatbush, and Graves-
end who had gathered to consider the defense and

welfare of the colonies. The English of the Long Island towns were the prime movers in this significant gathering. There is an unmistakable English flavor in the contention of *The Humble Remonstrance* adopted by the Convention, that "'tis contrary to the first intentions and genuine principles of every well regulated government, that one or more men should arrogate to themselves the exclusive power to dispose, at will, of the life and property of any individual." As a people "not conquered or subjugated, but settled here on a mutual covenant and contract entered into with the Lord Patroons, with the consent of the Natives," they protested against the enactment of laws and the appointment of magistrates without their consent or that of their representatives.

Stuyvesant replied with his usual bigotry and in a rage at being contradicted. He asserted that there was little wisdom to be expected from popular election when naturally "each would vote for one of his own stamp, the thief for a thief, the rogue, the tippler and the smuggler for his brother in iniquity, so that he may enjoy more latitude in vice and fraud." Finally Stuyvesant ordered the delegates to disperse, declaring: "We derive our authority from God and the Company, not from a few ignorant subjects, and we alone can call the inhabitants together."

With popular support thus alienated and with appeals for financial and military aid from the States-General and the West India Company denied or ignored, the end of New Netherland was clearly in sight. In 1663 Stuyvesant wrote to the Company begging them to send him reënforcements. "Otherwise," he said, "it is wholly out of our power to keep the sinking ship afloat any longer."

This year was full of omens. The valley of the Hudson was shaken by an earthquake followed by an overflow of the river, which ruined the crops. Smallpox visited the colony, and on top of all these calamities came the appalling Indian massacre at Esopus. The following year, 1664, brought the arrival of the English fleet, the declaration of war, and the surrender of the Dutch Province. For many years the English had protested against the Dutch claims to the territory on the North and South rivers. Their navigators had tried to contest the trade in furs, and their Government at home had interfered with vessels sailing to and from New Amsterdam. Now at length Charles II was ready to appropriate the Dutch possessions. He did not trouble himself with questions of international law, still less with international ethics; but, armed with the flimsy pretense that Cabot's visit established England's claim to the territory, he stealthily made preparations to seize the defenseless colony on the river which had begun to be known as the Hudson.

Five hundred veteran troops were embarked on four ships, under command of Colonel Richard Nicolls, and sailed on their expedition of conquest. Stuyvesant's suspicions, aroused by rumors of invasion, were so far lulled by dispatches from Holland that he allowed several ships at New Amsterdam to sail for Curaçao ladened with provisions, while he himself journeyed to Rensselaerswyck to quell an Indian outbreak. While he was occupied in this task, a messenger arrived to inform him that the English fleet was hourly expected in the harbor of New Amsterdam. Stuyvesant made haste down the river; but on the day after he arrived at Manhattan Island, he saw ships flying the flag of England in the lower harbor, where they anchored below the Narrows. Colonel Nicolls demanded the surrender of the "towns situate on the island commonly known by the name of Manhattoes, with all the forts thereunto belonging."

Although the case of New Amsterdam was now hopeless, Stuyvesant yet strove for delay. He sent a deputation to Nicolls to carry on a parley; but Nicolls was firm. "When may we visit you again?" the deputation asked. Nicolls replied with grim humor that he would speak with them at Manhattan. "Friends are welcome there," answered Stuyvesant's representative diplomatically; but Nicolls told them bluntly that he was coming with ships and soldiers. "Hoist a white flag at the fort," he said, "and I may consider your proposals."

Colonel Nicolls was as good as his word and, to the consternation of the dwellers in New Amsterdam, the fleet of English frigates, under full sail and with all guns loaded, appeared before the walls of the useless old Fort Amsterdam. Stuyvesant stood on one of the angles of the fort and the gunners with lighted matches awaited his command to fire. The people entreated him to yield. "Resistance is not soldiership," said one of them. "It is sheer madness." Stuyvesant, who with all his faults was a brave soldier, felt to the quick the humiliation; but he saw also that resistance meant only useless bloodshed. At last he submitted, and the English vessels sailed on their way unmolested, while Stuyvesant groaned, "I would much rather be carried to my grave."

Without firing a shot the English thus took possession of the rich country which the States-General had not thought worth defending, and New Netherland became New York.

CHAPTER V

BECAUSE the Netherlanders were not, like the New Englanders, fugitives from persecution at the hands of their fellow-countrymen, the Dutch colonization in America is often spoken of as a purely commercial venture; but in reality the founding of New Netherland marked a momentous epoch in the struggle for the freedom of conscience. Established between the long contest with the Inquisition in Spain and the Thirty Years' War for religious liberty in Germany, this plantation along the Hudson offered protection in America to those rights of free conscience for which so much blood had been shed and so much treasure spent in Europe.

The Dutch colonists were deeply religious, with no more bigotry than was inseparable from the ideas of the seventeenth century. They were determined to uphold the right to worship God in

their own way; and to say that their own way of
worship was as dear to them as their beliefs is not
strikingly to differentiate them from the rest of
mankind. They brought with them from the home
country a tenacious reverence for their fathers'
method of worship and for the Calvinistic polity
of the Dutch Reformed Church. They looked
with awe upon the *synod*, the final tribunal in
Holland for ecclesiastical disputes. They regarded
with respect the *classis*, composed of ministers and
elders in a certain district; but their hearts went
out in a special affection to the *consistory*, which
was made up of the ministers and elders of the
single local *kerk*. This at least they could repro-
duce in the crude conditions under which they
labored, and it seemed a link with the home which
they had left so far behind them.

They had no intention, however, of forcing this
church discipline on those who could not con-
scientiously accept it. The devout wish of William
the Silent that all his countrymen might dwell together in amity regardless of religious differences
was fulfilled among the early settlers in New
Netherland. Their reputation for tolerance was
spread abroad early in the history of the colony, and Huguenots, Lutherans, Presbyterians,

Moravians, and Anabaptists lived unmolested in New Netherland till the coming of Director Peter Stuyvesant in 1647.

The religious tyranny which marked Stuyvesant's rule must be set down to his personal discredit, for almost every instance of persecution was met by protest from the settlers themselves, including his coreligionists. He deported to Holland a Lutheran preacher; he revived and enforced a dormant rule of the West India Company which forbade the establishment of any church other than the Dutch Reformed; and he imprisoned parents who refused to have their children baptized in that faith. But it was in his dealings with the Quakers that his bigotry showed itself in its most despotic form. Robert Hodgson, a young Quaker, was arrested in Hempstead, Long Island, and was brought to New Amsterdam. After he had been kept in prison for several days, the magistrate condemned him either to pay a fine of a hundred guilders or to work with a wheelbarrow for two years in company with negroes. He declined to do either. After two or three days he was whipped on his bare back and warned that the punishment would be repeated if he persisted in his obstinacy. This treatment is recorded by the

Domines Megapolensis and Drisius in a letter to the *classis* of Amsterdam, not only without protest but with every sign of approbation. Yet in the end public opinion made itself felt and Mrs. Bayard, Stuyvesant's sister (or sister-in-law, as some authorities say) procured the release of his victim.

In another case, a resident of Flushing ventured to hold Quaker meetings at his home. He was sentenced to pay a fine or submit to be flogged and banished; but the town officers refused to carry out the decree. A letter, signed by a number of prominent townsfolk of Flushing, declared that the law of love, peace, and liberty was the true glory of Holland, that they desired not to offend one of Christ's little ones under whatever name he appeared, whether Presbyterian, Independent, Baptist, or Quaker. "Should any of these people come in love among us therefore," said they, "we cannot in conscience lay violent hands upon them." This letter immediately brought down upon the writers the despotic rage of Stuyvesant. The sheriff of Flushing was cashiered and fined; the town clerk was imprisoned; and penalties of varying degree were imposed on all the signers.

When accounts of Stuyvesant's proceedings

reached Amsterdam, however, he received from the Chamber a letter of stinging rebuke, informing him that "the consciences of men ought to be free and unshackled, so long as they continue moderate, inoffensive, and not hostile to government." The Chamber, after reminding the Director that toleration in old Amsterdam had brought the oppressed and persecuted of all countries to that city as to an asylum, recommended Stuyvesant to follow in the same course. Herewith ended the brief period of religious persecution in New Netherland.

The amiable Domine Megapolensis who acquiesced in these persecutions came over to the colony of Rensselaerswyck in 1642 in the service of Kiliaen Van Rensselaer. He was to have a salary of forty guilders per month and a fit dwelling that was to be provided for him. So the "Reverend, Pious, and learned Dr. Johannes Megapolensis, junior," set sail for America "to proclaim Christ to Christians and heathens in such distant lands." His name, by the way, like that of Erasmus, Melanchthon, Æcolampadius, Dryander, and other worthies of the Reformation, was a classical form of the homely Dutch patronymic to which he had been born.

Apparently the Reverend Johannes was more

successful in his mission to the heathen than in that to the Christians, for he learned the Mohawk language, wrote a valuable account of the tribe, and understood them better than he understood the Lutherans and Quakers of New Amsterdam and Long Island. In 1664 when Stuyvesant was in the mood to fire on the British fleet and take the consequences, Megapolensis, so tradition runs, dissuaded him with the argument: "Of what avail are our poor guns against that broadside of more than sixty? It is wrong to shed innocent blood." One wonders if the *domine* had any room in his mind for thoughts of the useless sufferings which had been inflicted on Hodgson and Townsend and the Lutheran preachers while he stood by consenting.

When Megapolensis arrived at New Netherland he found the Reverend Everardus Bogardus already installed as minister of the Gospel at Fort Amsterdam, his predecessor Michaelius having returned to Holland. From the beginning Bogardus proved a thorn in the side of the Government. He came to blows with Van Twiller and wrote a letter to the Director in which he called him a child of the Devil, a villain whose bucks were better than he, to whom he should give such a shake from the pulpit the following Sabbath as would make him shudder.

The difficulties which Bogardus had with Van Twiller, however, were as the breath of May zephyrs compared to his stormy quarrels with Kieft. This Director had taken Bogardus to task for having gone into the pulpit intoxicated, and had also accused him of defending the greatest criminals in the country and of writing in their defense. The fighting parson promptly countered on this attack. "What," he asked from the pulpit, "are the great men of the country but receptacles of wrath, fountains of woe and trouble? Nothing is thought of but to plunder other people's property — to dismiss — to banish — to transport to Holland." Kieft, realizing that he had raised up a fighter more unsparing than himself and, unable to endure these harangues from the pulpit, ceased to attend the *kerk;* but the warlike *domine* continued to belabor him till Kieft prepared an indictment, beginning: "Whereas your conduct stirs the people to mutiny and rebellion when they are already too much divided, causes schisms and abuses in the church, and makes us a scorn and a laughing stock to our neighbors, all which cannot be tolerated in a country where justice is maintained, therefore our sacred duty imperatively requires us to prosecute you in a court of justice." The quarrel was never fought to a finish but was allowed to die out, and the episode ended without credit to either party.

Like everything else in the colony of New Netherland, the original meeting-places for worship were of the simplest type. Domine Megapolensis held services in his own house, and Bogardus conducted worship in the upper part of the horse-mill at Fort Amsterdam, where before his arrival Sebastian Jansen Krol and Jan Huyck had read from the Scriptures on Sunday. These men had been appointed *ziekentroosters* or *krankenbesoeckers* (*i.e.*, consolers of the sick), whose business it was, in addition to their consolatory functions, to hold Sunday services in the absence of a regularly ordained clergyman. In time these rude gathering-places gave way to buildings of wood or stone, modeled, as one would expect, on similar buildings in the old country, with a pulpit built high above the congregation, perhaps with intent to emphasize the authority of the church.

The clerk, or *voorleser*, standing in the baptistery below the pulpit, opened the services by reading from the Bible and leading in the singing of a psalm. The *domine*, who had stood in silent prayer during the psalm, afterward entered the pulpit, and then laid out his text and its connection with the sermon to follow — a part of the service known as the *exordium remotum*. During this address the deacons stood facing the pulpit, alms-bag in hand. The deacons collected the contribution by thrusting in front of each row of seats the *kerk sacjes* of cloth or velvet suspended from the end of a long pole. Sometimes a bell hung at the bottom of the bag to call the attention of the slothful or the niggardly to the contribution, and while the bags were passed the *domine* was wont to dwell upon the necessities of the poor and to invoke blessings upon those who gave liberally to their support. When the sermon commenced, the *voorsinger* turned the hour-glass which marked the length of the discourse. The sermon ended, the *voorleser* rose and, with the aid of a long rod cleft in the end, handed to the *domine* in the pulpit the requests for prayers or thanksgiving offered by members of the congregation. When these had been read aloud, another psalm was sung and the people then filed out in an orderly procession.

The principle of competitive giving for the church was evidently well understood in New

Amsterdam. De Vries has left us an account of a conversation held in 1642 between himself and Kieft in which he told the Director that there was great need of a church, that it was a scandal when the English came that they should see only a mean barn for public worship, that the first thing built in New England after the dwellings was a church, and that there was the less excuse for the Dutch as they had fine wood, good stone, and lime made from oyster shells, close at hand. The Director admitted the justice of the plea but asked who would undertake the work. "Those who love the Reformed Religion," De Vries answered. Kieft replied adroitly that De Vries must be one of them, as he had proposed the plan, and that he should give a hundred guilders. De Vries craftily observed that Kieft as commander must be the first giver. Kieft bethought himself that he could use several thousand guilders from the Company's funds. Not only was he as good as his word, but later he contrived to extort private subscriptions on the occasion of the marriage of Bogardus's stepdaughter. As usual when the *domine* was present, the wine flowed freely. "The Director thought this a good time for his purpose, and set to work after the fourth or fifth drink; and he himself setting a liberal example, let the wedding-guests sign whatever they were disposed to give towards the church. Each, then, with a light head, subscribed away at a handsome rate, one competing with the other; and although some heartily repented it when their senses came back, they were obliged nevertheless to pay."

In view of this story it was perhaps a fine irony which inspired the inscription placed on the church when it was finished: "Ao. Do. MDCXLII. W. Kieft Dr. Gr. *Heeft de Gemeente desen Tempel doen Bouwen*," *i.e.*, "William Kieft, the Director-General, has caused the congregation to build this church." The correct interpretation, however, probably read: "William Kieft being Director-General, the congregation has caused this church to be built." [1]

Evidently religion prospered better than education in the colony, for the same lively witness who reports the Bogardus affair and the generosity stimulated by the flowing wine says also: "The bowl has been passed around a long time for a common school which has been built with words, for as yet the first stone is not laid; some materials only have been provided. However the money

[1] Brodhead, *History of the State of New York*, vol. I, p. 337 (note).

given for the purpose has all disappeared and is mostly spent, so that it falls somewhat short; and nothing permanent has as yet been effected for this purpose."

The first schoolmaster sent to New Netherland arrived in 1633 at the same time as Bogardus, and represented the cause of education even less creditably than did the bibulous *domine* that of religion. Adam Roelantsen was twenty-seven years old when he was sent over seas as instructor of youth in the colony, and he was as precious a scoundrel as ever was set to teach the young. He eked out his slender income in the early days by taking in washing or by establishing a bleachery, which must be noted as one of the most creditable items in his scandalous career. He was constantly before the local courts of New Amsterdam, sometimes as plaintiff, sometimes as defendant, and finally he appeared as a malefactor charged with so grave an offense that the court declared that, as such deeds could not be tolerated, "therefore we condemn the said Roelantsen to be brought to the place of execution and there flogged and banished forever out of this country." Apparently, on the plea of having four motherless children, he escaped the infliction of punishment and continued alternately

to amuse and to outrage the respectable burghers
of New Amsterdam. He was succeeded in order by
Jan Stevensen, Jan Cornelissen, William Verstius,
sometimes written Vestens, Johannes Morice de la
Montagne, Harmanus Van Hoboocken, and Evert
Pietersen. In addition to these there were two
teachers of a Latin school and several unofficial
instructors.

The duties of these early teachers were by no
means light, especially in proportion to their scanty
wage. We learn in one case that school began at
eight in the morning and lasted until eleven, when
there was a two-hour recess, after which it began
again at one and closed at four o'clock. It was the
duty of the teacher to instruct the children in the
catechism and common prayer. The teacher was
ordered to appear at the church on Wednesdays
with the children entrusted to his care, to examine
his scholars "in the presence of the Reverend
Ministers and Elders who may be present, what
they in the course of the week, do remember of
the Christian commands and catechism, and what
progress they have made; after which the children
shall be allowed a decent recreation."

Besides his duties as instructor, the official
schoolmaster was pledged "to promote religious

worship, to read a portion of the word of God to the people, to endeavor, as much as possible to bring them up in the ways of the Lord, to console them in their sickness, and to conduct himself with all diligence and fidelity in his calling, so as to give others a good example as becometh a devout, pious and worthy consoler of the sick, church-clerk, Precenter and School master."

Throughout the history of New Netherland we find the church and school closely knit together. Frequently the same building served for secular instruction on week-days and for religious service on Sundays. In a letter written by Van Curler to his patroon, he says: "As for the Church it is not yet contracted for, nor even begun. . . . That which I intend to build this summer in the pine grove (or green wood) will be thirty-four feet long by nineteen wide. It will be large enough for the first three or four years to preach in and can afterwards always serve for the residence of the *sexton* or for a school."

How small were the assemblies of the faithful in the early days we may gather from a letter of Michaelius, the first *domine* of the colony, incidentally also one of the most lovable and spiritually minded of these men. In his account of the condition of the church at Manhattan he observes that at the first communion fifty were present. The number of Walloons and French-speaking settlers was so small that the *domine* did not think it worth while to hold a special service for them, but once in four months he contented himself with administering the communion and preaching a sermon in French. This discourse he found it necessary to commit to writing, as he could not trust himself to speak extemporaneously in that language. There is something beautiful and pathetic in the picture of this little group of half a hundred settlers in the wilderness, gathered in the upper room of the grist-mill, surrounded by the sacks of grain, and drinking from the *avondmaalsbeker*, or communion cup, while the rafters echoed to the solemn sounds of the liturgy which had been familiar in their old homes across the sea.

There is the true ring of a devout and simple piety in all the utterances of the settlers on the subject of their church. The pioneers were ready to spend and be spent in its service and they gave freely out of their scanty resources for its support. In the matter of education their enthusiasm, as we have seen, was far less glowing, and the reasons for this coolness are a subject for curious consideration. The Dutch in Europe were a highly cultivated people, devoted to learning and reverencing the printed book. Why then were their countrymen in the New World willing to leave the education of their children in the hands of inferior teachers and to delay so long the building of suitable schoolhouses?

We must remember that the colonists in the early days were drawn from a very simple class. Their church was important to them as a social center as well as a spiritual guide. For this church they were willing to make any sacrifice; but that done, they must pause and consider the needs of their daily life. Children old enough to attend school were old enough to lend a helping hand on the *bouwerie*, in the dairy, or by the side of the cradle. Money if plentiful might well be spent on salaries and schoolhouses; but if scarce, it must be saved for bread and butter, clothing, warmth, and shelter. In short, reading, writing, and figuring could wait; but souls must be saved first; and after that eating and drinking were matters of pressing urgency. Fortunately, however, not all education is bound up in books, and, in the making of sturdy and efficient colonists, the rude training of hardships and privation when combined with a first-hand knowledge of nature and of the essential industries provided a fair substitute for learning.

On the other side of the picture we must consider what type of men would naturally be drawn to cross the sea and settle in the new colony as schoolmasters. Many of the clergymen came urged by the same zeal for the conversion of the savages which fired John Eliot in New England and the Jesuit Fathers in the Canadian missions. For the schoolmasters there was not this incentive, and they naturally looked upon the question of emigration as a business enterprise or a chance of professional advancement. As a first consideration they must have realized that they were leaving a country where education and educators were held in high respect. "There was hardly a Netherlander," says Motley, "man, woman or child, that could not read and write. The school was the common property of the people, paid for among the municipal expenses in the cities as well as in the rural districts. There were not only common schools but classical schools. In the burgher families it was rare to find boys who had not been taught Latin or girls unacquainted with French." From this atmosphere of scholastic enthusiasm, from the opportunities of the libraries and contact with the universities, the pedagogue was invited to turn to a rude settlement in the primeval forest, where the Bible, the catechism, and the concordance formed the greater part of the literary wealth at his disposal, and to take up the multiple duties of sexton, bell-ringer, precentor, schoolmaster, consoler of the sick, and general understudy for the *domine*. In return for this he was to receive scanty wages in either cash or public esteem.

What hardships were experienced by these early schoolmasters in New Netherland we may understand by reading the *Reverential Request* written by Harmanus Van Hoboocken to the burgomasters and *schepens* that he may be allowed the use of the hall and side-chamber of the *Stadt-Huys* to accommodate his school and as a residence for his family, as he has no place to keep school in or to live in during the winter, for it is necessary that the rooms should be made warm, and that cannot be done in his own house. The burgomasters and *schepens* replied that "whereas the room which petitioner asks for his use as a dwelling and schoolroom is out of repair and moreover is wanted for other uses it cannot be allowed to him. But as the town youth are doing so uncommon well now, it is thought proper to find a convenient place for their accommodation and for that purpose petitioner is granted one hundred guilders yearly."

Can we wonder that New Netherland did not secure a particularly learned and distinguished type of pedagogue in the early days? In 1658 the burgomasters and *schepens* of New Amsterdam with a view to founding an academy petitioned the West India Company for a teacher of Latin, and Alexander Carolus Curtius was sent over to be the classical teacher in the new academy; but he was so disheartened by the smallness of his salary and by the roughness of the youthful burghers that he shortly returned to Holland, and his place was taken by Ægidius Luyck, who, though only twenty-two years old, established such discipline and taught so well that the reputation of the academy spread far and wide, and Dutch boys were no longer sent to New England to learn their classics.

CHAPTER VI

THE BURGHERS

In the earliest days of New Netherland there were no *burgers* because, as the name implies, burghers are town-dwellers, and for a number of years after the coming of the Dutch nothing worthy to be called a town existed in the colony. In the middle of the seventeenth century a traveler wrote from New Netherland that there were only three towns on the Hudson — Fort Orange, Rondout, and New Amsterdam — and that the rest were mere villages or settlements.

These centers were at first trading-posts, and it is as idle to judge of the manners, customs, and dress prevailing in them by those of Holland at the same epoch, as to judge San Francisco in the mining days of 1849 by Boston and New York at the same date. These early traders and settlers brought with them the character and traditions of home; but their way of life was perforce modified by the crude conditions into which they plunged. The picturesque farmhouses of Long Island and the crow-gables of New Amsterdam were not built in a day. Savages must be subdued and land cleared and planted before the evolution of the dwelling could fairly begin. Primitive community life lingered long even on Manhattan Island. As late as 1649 the farmers petitioned for a free pasturage between their plantation of Schepmoes and the fence of the Great Bowerie Number One. The City Hall Park region bounded by Broadway, Nassau, Ann, and Chambers Streets continued very late to be recognized as village commons where the cattle were pastured. The cowherd drove the cows afield and home again at milking-time, and it was his business to sound his horn at every gate announcing the safe return of the cows. Correspondingly in the morning the harsh summons called the cattle from every yard to join the procession toward the meadows.

When Tienhoven, Stuyvesant's secretary, sent out information for the benefit of those planning to take up land in New Netherland, he suggested that those who had not means to build at first might shelter themselves by digging a pit six or seven feet deep as large as needed, covering the

floor and walls with timber and placing over it a
roof of spars covered with bark or green sods.
Even with this rude housing he suggests planting
at once a garden with all sorts of pot-herbs and
maize, or Indian corn, which might serve as food
for man and beast alike. Naturally these pioneer
conditions of living lasted longer in the farming
region than at New Amsterdam, where as early as
1640 we see simple but comfortable little houses
clustered in the shelter of the fort, and gathered
close about the stone tavern, the West India Company's stores, and the Church of St. Nicholas.
The gallows and pillory, in full view, seemed to
serve notice that law and order had asserted themselves and that settlers might safely solidify their
houses and holdings.

In 1648 the building of wooden chimneys was
forbidden, and roofs of reed were replaced with
more solid and less inflammable material. The
constant threat of fire led to drastic regulations
for the cleaning of chimneys. It was ordered that
"if anyone prove negligent he shall, whenever the
Firewardens find the chimneys foul, forthwith
without any contradiction, pay them a fine of three
guilders for every flue found on examination to be
dirty, to be expended for fire ladders, hooks and

buckets, which shall be procured and provided at the earliest and most convenient opportunity."

The early settlers found much difficulty in enforcing public sanitation, for, in spite of the world-wide reputation of the Dutch for indoor cleanliness, we find the burghers in 1658 bitterly reproached for throwing their rubbish, filth, dead animals, and the like into the streets "to the great inconvenience of the community and dangers arising from it." The burgomasters and *schepens* ordained that all such refuse be brought to dumping-grounds near the City Hall and the gallows or to other designated places. Failure to observe this rule was punishable by fines or severer penalties.

As prosperity increased, all conditions of living improved. Many ships from Holland brought loads of brick and tiles as ballast, and the houses began to assume the typical Dutch aspect. They were still built chiefly of wood, but with a gable end of brick facing the street. The steep roofs seldom had eave-troughs, at least in the early days, and mention is made in deeds of "free-drip."

The house was supplied, as the chronicler tells us, with "an abundance of large doors and small windows on every floor, the date of its erection was curiously designated by iron figures on the front, and on the top of the roof was perched a fierce little weather-cock to let the family into the important secret which way the wind blew." The front doors were usually divided, as in the old houses in Holland, into an upper and lower half hung on heavy hinges. The door opened with a latch, and bore a brass knocker wrought frequently in the device of an animal's head.

Only on formal occasions was this door thrown open or the fore-room to which it gave access used, for the life of the family, as in all primitive communities, was centered in the kitchen. Here in winter roared the great fires up the wide-throated chimneys. Here children and negro servants gathered in groups and told stories of the old home and the new. Here the women knit their stockings and here the burghers smoked when the day's work was done. But the fore-room, or *voorhuis*, though seldom occupied, was dear to the soul of the *vrouw* of New Netherland. Here stood all the treasures too valuable or too fragile for daily use: the *kast*, or chest, stored with household linen, the cabinet filled with Delft plates from Holland, and generally the carved four-poster covered with feather beds of prime goose-feathers and hung with gay chintz.

A shrewd observer has said that luxury implies waste while comfort lives in thrift. We are safe in assuming that comfort rather than luxury prevailed in New Netherland and that the highly colored pictures of elegant life on the shores of the Hudson represent a very late phase, when the Dutch influence still prevailed under English protection. The earlier settlers were a far simpler people, whose floors were scrubbed and sanded instead of carpeted, who used hour-glasses instead of clocks, and who set their four-poster beds in the rooms where visitors were formally received.

It was of course the "great burghers" who set the social as well as the official tone in New Amsterdam.[1] It was they who owned the finest houses,

---

[1] In 1657 the burgomasters and *schepens* were authorized to create a great *burger-recht* the members of which should be in a sense a privileged class. It was set forth that "whereas in all beginnings some thing or person must be the first so that afterward a distinction may take place, in like manner it must be in establishing the great and small citizenship." For which reason the line of great burghers was drawn as follows: first, those who had been members of the supreme government; second, the burgomasters and *schepens* of the city past and present; third, ministers of the gospel; fourth, officers of the militia from the staff to the ensign included. The privileges of this caste were open to the male descendants of each class; but as they could be secured by others outside the sacred circle on payment of fifty guilders it is difficult to understand wherein the exclusiveness lay. The small burghers were decreed to be those who had lived in the city for a year and six weeks and had kept fire and light, those born within the town,

who imported tables and chests of ebony inlaid
with ivory. It was they whose wives were bravely
fitted out with petticoats, over which an upper
garment was looped to display the velvet, cloth,
silk, or satin which marked the social position and
material wealth of the wearer. The burgher himself went clad, according to his wealth, in cloaks
of cloth or velvet, embroidered or silk-lined; but
he always wore wide boots and wide breeches and a
coat adorned with an abundance of buttons, the
whole topped by a broad-brimmed hat adorned
with buckles and feathers and seldom removed
in the house. The dress of the farmers was simpler
than that of the town-dwellers or burghers. It
consisted generally of wide breeches, a *hemdrok*
or shirt-coat made of wool or cotton, an overfrock
called a *paltsrok*, a low flat collar, the usual wide-
brimmed hat, and shoes of leather on Sundays, and
of wood on week-days for work on the *bouwerie*.
The children of burghers and farmers alike were
clad in miniature copies of the garb of their elders,
doubtless in many cases wearing the same garments

and those who had married the daughters of citizens. A payment of
twenty guilders was exacted of all such. This effort to promote class
distinctions was soon abandoned. In 1668 the distinction was abolished and every burgher, on payment of fifty guilders, was declared
ntitled to all burgher privileges.

made over by removing the outworn portions. It was a question of warmth rather than fashion which confronted the settlers and their children.

To those of us who believe that the state exists for the protection of the home and the home for the protection of the child, it is neither futile nor frivolous to consider at some length what life had to offer to the small colonists. Little Sarah Rapaelje, "the first-born Christian daughter in New Netherland," was soon surrounded by a circle of boys and girls. Cornelis Maasen and his wife came over in 1631, and their first child was born on the voyage. Following this little Hendrick came Martin, Maas, Steyntje, and Tobias. We have already noted the two little motherless daughters of Domine Michaelius who were so hard put to it for a nurse. A little later came Domine Megapolensis with his children Hellegond, Dirrick, Jan, and Samuel, running from eight to fourteen years in age. The patroon had directed that they be furnished with clothing "in such small and compact parcels as can be properly stowed away on the ship."

With the era of permanent settlers in New Netherland, cradles came to be in demand. In the region of New Amsterdam the familiar hooded variety was brought from Holland, while farther up the river and especially among the poorer folk birch bark was fashioned into a sleeping-place for the babies. For the older children trundle-beds fitting under the big four-posters of the elders and rolled out at night were much in use, since the difficulty of heating made economy of bedroom-space a necessity. This *treke-bed* and its protecting four-poster, however, probably came later than the built-in *sloep-bank*, little more than a bunk in the side of the wall concealed by a curtain and softened by thick feather-beds.

However rude the sleeping-place of the babies, the old home lullabies soothed them to slumber. Dearest and most familiar was the following:

> Trip a trop a tronjes,
> De varken in de boonjes,
> De koejes in de klaver,
> De paaden in de haver,
> De eenjes in de water plas,
> De kalver in de lang gras,
> So groot myn klein poppetje was.

Thus to pictures of pigs in the bean patch and cows in the clover, ducks in the water and calves in the meadow, the little ones fell peacefully to sleep, oblivious of the wild beasts and wilder men lurking in the primeval forests around the little clearing where the pioneers were making a home for themselves and their children.

When the babies' eyelids unclosed in the morning they opened on a busy scene, for whatever anxious vigils the father and mother might have kept through the night, toil began with the dawn. The boys were set to gathering firewood and drawing water, while the *goede vrouw* was busily preparing a substantial morning meal of suppawn and sausage before her husband began the day's work of loading beaver-skins or tilling the ground or hewing timber. A pioneer life means hard work for children as well as for their elders, and in the early years there was little time for play on the part of the youthful New Netherlanders. As prosperity advanced and as negro servants were introduced, the privileges of childhood were extended and we find accounts of their sliding on their *slees* or sleds down the hills of Fort Orange and skating at New Amsterdam on the Collect Pond, which took its name from the Dutch *kalk*, or lime, and was so called from the heaps of oyster-shells accumulated by the Indians. The skates were of the type used in Holland, very long with curves at the front and rear, and, when metal could not be obtained, formed of ox-bone.

With an appetite bred of out-of-door work and play, and a breakfast hour at five or six in the morning, the children were hungry for the homely and substantial dinner when it eventually appeared at early noon. Whatever social visits were planned took place at the supper, which occurred between three o'clock and six. The tea-table, the chronicler tells us,

was crowned with a huge earthen dish, well stored with slices of fat pork and fried trout, cut up into morsels and swimming in gravy. The company, being seated round the genial board and each furnished with a fork, evinced their dexterity in launching at the fattest pieces in this mighty dish in much the same manner as sailors harpoon porpoises at sea, or our Indians spear salmon in the lakes.

Sometimes the table was graced with immense apple pies, or saucers full of preserved peaches or pears; but it was always sure to boast an enormous dish of balls of sweetened dough, fried in hog's fat and called doughnuts or *olykoeks*. . . . The tea was served out of a majestic Delft tea-pot ornamented with paintings of fat little Dutch shepherds and shepherdesses tending pigs, with boats sailing in the air and houses built in the clouds. . . . To sweeten the beverage a lump of sugar was laid beside each cup and the company alternately nibbled and sipped with great decorum.

In the houses of the richer colonists, as prosperity advanced, shell-shaped silver boxes for sugar, called "bite and stir" boxes, were set on the table and, according to one authority, the lumps of sugar were of the nature of toffy with molasses added to the sugar.

The feast ended, the young folk went their homeward way lighted by the moon, or, late in the century, on dark nights by a lantern hung on a pole from every seventh house. When the curfew rang from the belfry "eight o'clock," lights were put out and all was made fast for the night, while the children's minds were set at rest by the tramp of the *klopperman*, who shook his rattle at each door as he passed from house to house through the dark hours, assuring the burghers that all was well and that no marauders were about.

If winter offered sports and pastimes, spring, summer, and autumn had each its own pleasures, fishing and clam digging, shooting and trapping, games with ball and slings, berry picking, and the gathering of peaches which fell so thickly that the very hogs refused them. The market days in New Amsterdam offered a long procession of delights to the young colonists. But merriest of all were the holidays which were observed in New Netherland after much the same fashion as in the old home.

8

I do not know how to account for the fact that while the struggle of the Dutch people with the Papacy had been as bitter as that of England and the throwing off of the yoke by the Dutch fully as decided, they still retained the holidays which the Puritans eschewed as dangerous remnants of superstition. Perhaps it was on the principle of robbing Satan of his hoofs and horns but keeping his cheerful scarlet costume, or perhaps they thought, as Rowland Hill remarked, that "it was poor policy to leave all the good times to the Devil." In any case it was all grist to the children's mill.

On the 1st of January all was arranged for the greeting of the New Year. Mighty bowls of punch were brewed, cordials prepared from long-cherished family recipes were brought out, and the women, in their best apparel, seated themselves in the seldom-used *ontvangkamer*, where wine was handed to their callers to be received with the wish of a "Happy New Year!" While these stately ceremonies were in progress the young people amused themselves with turkey-shooting, sleigh-riding, skating, and dancing.

After New Year's Day the most characteristic national and local holiday was *Pinkster*, coming in the seventh week after *Paasch*, or Easter, and falling generally in late May or early June. The orchards were then white with blossoms and the grass thick with dandelions and spring flowers. Children set out early to gather boughs from the green woods. These boughs they sprinkled with water and left over the doors of late sleepers that the sluggards might be drenched on opening the door. At first all was innocent merriment, gathering of Pinkster flowers, and picnicking; but for some unexplained reason this festival was gradually relegated to the negroes. Apple-jack was freely consumed, barbaric dances began, and fun so far degenerated into license that the white people and their children shunned the festivity.

The *Kermis*, an Old World festival, was one of those early introduced at New Amsterdam. It originated centuries before and had taken its name from the *kerk mis* or church mass. In the olden days it was celebrated with pomp and solemnity, but it early developed a more festive character. Booths and stalls were erected for a market, and dances and processions were organized. The first stroke of the clock at noon opened at the same moment the market and the first dance. The last stroke saw white crosses nailed on all the bridges across the canal and on the market place. It was indeed a festive appearance that the market presented, with its double stalls filled with eggs and gherkins, its booths hung with dried fish, its *poffertjeskraam* dispensing the tempting batter-cakes, and its *wafelkraamen* offering the more costly and aristocratic waffles. The youths and maidens were given full license to parade arm in arm along the streets singing "Hossen, hossen, hossen!" and making the town ring with their mirth and laughter. The first *Kermis* held at New Amsterdam was in October, 1659. Booths were arranged on the parade ground, and barter and sale and merrymaking went on gaily for six weeks, to the unspeakable joy of the little Hendricks and Jans and Annetjes who wandered from booth to booth.

But keen as the delight of the Dutch children may have been, there was in their minds the hope of even better things to come a few weeks later, at their own especial, particular, undisputed feast of St. Nicholas, the beloved Santa Claus, patron saint of children in general and of young Netherlanders in particular. The 6th of December was the day dedicated to this genial benefactor, and on the eventful night a white sheet was spread on the floor. Around this stood the children singing

songs of welcome, of which the most popular was
the familiar

> Saint Nicholaes, goed heilig man,
> Trekt uw'besten tabbard aan,
> En reist daamee naar Amsterdam,
> Von Amsterdam naar Spanje.

If the Saint would ride forth thus accoutered and
if he would do what they asked of him, the children
explained that they would be his good friends, as
for that matter they always had been, and would
serve him as long as they lived. At last the fateful
moment arrived. A shower of sweets was hurled
through the open door and amid the general
scramble appeared the Saint in full vestments
attended by a servant known as *Knecht Ruprecht*,
and, after the Dutch settlements in America, a
black man, who added much to the fascination and
excitement of the occasion. He held in one hand
an open sack into which to put particularly ill-
behaved children, while in the other hand he
carried a bunch of rods, which he shook vigorously
from time to time. The good Saint meanwhile
smilingly distributed to the children the parcels
that he had brought, and, after these had all been
opened and the presents had been sufficiently

admired, the children dropped into their trundle-beds to dream of all the glories of the day.

When the dust-sheet and litter of wrappings had been removed, the older people gathered around a table spread with a white cloth and set out with chocolate punch and a dish of steaming hot chestnuts, while the inevitable pipe, ornamented with a head of St. Nicholas, made its appearance and the evening ended with dancing and song in honor of the "goed heilig man."

Besides these stated anniversaries, home life had its more intimate festivities such as those celebrating the birth of a child, whose christening was made quite a solemn event. Every church owned its *doop-becken* or dipping bowl from which the water was taken to be dropped on the baby's head. One beautiful bowl of silver dating from the year 1695 is still in existence in a New York church. About a week after the birth of the little New Netherlander, the neighbors were summoned to rejoice with the proud father and mother. In the early days of the colony and in the farming region, these gatherings were as rude and simple as they were under similar conditions in Holland. The men were invited at noon to partake of a long pipe and a bottle of gin and bitters. The women arrived

later to find spread for their entertainment dishes
of rusks spread with aniseed and known as *muisjes*
or mice, accompanied by eggnog. As society
grew more sophisticated in the colony, these simple
gatherings gave place to the elaborate caudle
parties, where the caudle was served in silver
bowls hung about with spoons that each guest
might ladle out for himself into a china cup the
rich compound of lemons, raisins, and spiced wine.

It is evident that there was no lack of material
good cheer among the colonists of New Netherland,
and we may be sure that the boys and girls secured
their share of substantials and dainties. I fear
they were rather rough and rude, these young
burghers, for all the reports which we have of them
show them always in conflict with law and order.
The boys especially, owing to deficient schooling
facilities, were quite out of hand. They set dogs
upon the night watchman at New Amsterdam and
shouted "Indians!" to frighten him in his rounds.
They tore the clothes from each other's backs in
the schoolroom where the unfortunate master was
striving to keep order. In Fort Orange sliding
became so fast and furious that the legislators were
obliged to threaten the confiscation of the *slees,*
and it was no doubt with a keen realization of the

behavior of their offspring that the inhabitants of
Flatbush inserted these words in the articles of
agreement with the new schoolmaster: "He shall
demean himself patient and friendly towards
the children and be active and attentive to their
improvement."

However little learning from books entered into
the lives of the young colonists, much that was
stimulating to the imagination came to them by
word of mouth from the *wilden*, from the negroes,
and from their elders as they sat about the blazing
fire in the twilight, or *schemerlicht*. Then the tales
were told of phantom ships, of ghosts walking on
the cliffs of the Highlands, and of the unlucky
wight who found his death in the river where he
had sworn to plunge in spite of the Devil, a spot
which still bears the name of Spuyten Duyvil in
memory of the rash boast.

We may find it hard to reconcile the reputation
of the Dutch as a phlegmatic and unimaginative
people with the fact that they and their children
endowed the Hudson with more glamour, more of
the supernatural and of elfin lore than haunts any
other waterway in America. Does the explana-
tion perhaps lie in the fact that the Dutch colonists,
coming from a small country situated on a level

plain where the landscape was open as far as the eye could see, and left no room for mystery, were suddenly transplanted to a region shut in between overhanging cliffs where lightning flashed and thunder rolled from mountain wall to mountain wall, where thick forests obscured the view, and strange aboriginal savages hid in the underbrush? Was it not the sense of wonder springing from this change in their accustomed surroundings that peopled the dim depths of the *hinterland* with shapes of elf and goblin, of demons and superhuman presences?

At any rate the spirit of mystery lurked on the outskirts of the Dutch settlements, and the youthful burghers along the Hudson were fed full on tales, mostly of a terrifying nature, drawn from the folklore of three races, the Dutch, the Indians, and the Africans, with some few strands interwoven from local legend and tradition that had already grown up along the banks of the Hudson.

It was a simple but by no means a pitiable life that was led in those days by burghers and farmers alike on the shores of this great river. Never does the esteemed Diedrich Knickerbocker come nearer the truth than when he says: "Happy would it have been for New Amsterdam could it always have existed in this state of blissful ignorance and lowly simplicity; but alas! the days of childhood are too sweet to last. Cities, like men, grow out of them in time and are doomed alike to grow into the bustle, the cares and the miseries of the world."

CHAPTER VII

MACHIAVELLI observed that to the wise ruler only two courses were open — to conciliate or to crush. The history of the Dutch in America illustrates by application the truth of this view. The settlers at Fort Orange conciliated the Indians and by this means not only lived in peace with the native tribes but established a bulwark between themselves and the French. Under Stuyvesant the settlers at Fort Amsterdam took a determined stand against the Swedes and crushed their power in America. Toward the English, however, the Dutch adopted a course of feeble aggression unbacked by force. Because they met English encroachments with that most fatal of all policies, protest without action, the Empire of the United Netherlands in America was blotted from the map.

The neighbors of the Dutch in America were the Indians, the French, the Swedes, and the English.

The earliest, most intimate, and most continuous relations of the Dutch settlers were with the Indians. These people were divided into a number of independent tribes or nations. The valley of the North River was shared by the Mohawks, who inhabited the region along the west side of its upper waters, and the Mohegans, or Mahicans, as the Dutch called them, who lived on either side of the banks of its lower reaches, with various smaller tribes scattered between. The warlike Manhattans occupied the island called by their name, while the Mohegans raised their wigwams also on the eastern shore of the upper river opposite the Mohawks, and ranged over the land reaching to the Connecticut River.

The Mohawks, with the Oneidas, the Onondagas, the Cayugas, and the Senecas, formed the famous Five Nations, generally known as the Iroquois. Their territory was bounded on the north by Lake Ontario and the St. Lawrence River, on the east by Lake Champlain and the North River, on the west by Lake Erie and the Niagara River, and on the south by the region occupied by the Lenni Lenape, or Delaware tribes. But their power extended far beyond these limits over dependent tribes. They were in a constant state of warfare with their Algonquin neighbors on the north and east, who had been enabled to offer a formidable resistance by the use of firearms furnished them by the French.

When, therefore, the white men appeared among the Mohawks, bearing these strange weapons which had been used with such dire effect against the Iroquois by the Algonquins, the Mohawks eagerly sought the friendship of the newcomers, hoping to secure the same power which had made their enemies triumphant. The Dutch were intelligent enough to make instant use of these friendly sentiments on the part of the natives and hastened to make a treaty with the Iroquois, the Mohegans, and the Lenni Lenapes.

This treaty, which is said to have been signed on the banks of Norman's Kill in the neighborhood of Albany, was concluded with all formalities. Each tribe was represented by its chief. The calumet was smoked, the hatchet was buried, and everlasting friendship was sworn between the old inhabitants and the new. By this agreement the Dutch secured not only peace with the neighboring Indians — a peace never broken in the north, whatever broils disturbed the lower waters of the river — but at the same time a guard between them and any encroachments of the French and Algonquins in Canada.

On the other boundaries and outskirts of their possessions, the Dutch were less fortunate. They had always claimed all the territory from the South or Delaware River to the Fresh or Connecticut River, but their pretensions were early challenged by the English on the ground of prior discovery and by the Swedes on the argument of non-occupation of the land.

The reports of the wealth to be acquired from the fur trade had quickly spread from Holland to Sweden, and as early as 1624, Gustavus Adolphus, encouraged by William Usselinx, a Dutchman and promoter of the Dutch West India Company, was planning expeditions to the New World. But the entrance of Sweden into the Thirty Years' War in 1630 put a stop to this plan, and the funds were applied to war purposes. Gustavus Adolphus fell at Lützen in 1632, leaving the kingdom to his little daughter Christina. Her Government was conducted by Oxenstiern, a statesman trained in the great traditions of Gustavus, who felt with him that an American colony would be "the jewel of his kingdom." An instrument for his purpose presented itself in Peter Minuit, who had returned to Holland in 1632, smarting under his dismissal as Director of New Netherland. He offered his services to Sweden for the establishment of a new colony, and they were accepted. In the opening of 1638, he arrived in what is now Delaware Bay with two ships, the *Griffin* and the *Key of Kalmar*. From the Indians he bought large tracts of land in what is now the State of Delaware, and on the site of the present city of Wilmington he planted a fort named Christina.

When news was brought to Kieft that Minuit had sailed up the South River and planned to raise the Swedish flag on a fort upon its shores, the Director promptly dispatched the following letter:

I, Willem Kieft, Director-General of New Netherland, residing in the island of Manhattan, in the Fort Amsterdam, under the government of the High and Mighty States-General of the United Netherlands and the West India Company, privileged by the Senate Chamber in Amsterdam, make known to thee, Peter Minuit, who stylest thyself commander in the service of Her Majesty, the Queen of Sweden, that the whole South River of New Netherland, both upper and lower, has been our property for many years, occupied with our forts, and sealed by our blood, which also was done when thou wast in the service of New Netherland, and is therefore well known to thee. But as thou art come between our forts to erect a fort to our damage and injury, which we will never permit, as we also believe Her Swedish Majesty hath not empowered thee to erect fortifications on our coasts and rivers, or to settle people on the lands adjoining or to undertake any other thing to our prejudice; now therefore we protest against all such encroachments and all the evil consequences from the same, as bloodshed, sedition and whatever injury our trading company may suffer, and declare that we shall protect our rights in every manner that may be advisable.

This blustering protest Minuit treated with contempt and continued building his fort. The Swedish colony soon grew so rapidly as to be a serious menace to the Dutch in spite of their stronger fortifications.

In 1642 Johan Printz, a lieutenant-colonel of cavalry, was sent over as Governor of New Sweden with instructions to maintain friendly relations with the Dutch, but to yield no foot of ground. He established several other settlements on the South or Delaware River. So tactlessly, however, did he perform his duties, that conflicts with the Dutch grew more and more frequent. He built two forts on opposite sides of the river and ordered that every ship entering the waters should strike her colors and await permission to pass. The first vessel on which the new orders were tried carried as a passenger David de Vries. The skipper asked his advice about lowering his colors. "If it were my ship," De Vries asserts that he answered, "I would not lower to these intruders." But peace at any price prevailed, the skipper lowered his colors, and the ship passed on to New Gottenburg, the capital of the colony. Here De Vries was welcomed by Governor Printz, whom the traveler describes as "a brave man of brave size." The evening was spent in talk over a jug of Rhenish wine. Such friendly intercourse and the aggressions of the English against both Dutch and Swedes led to the temporary alliance of these latter in 1651. Indians called in council confirmed the Dutch title to all lands except the site of the Swedish fort planted by Minuit, and a peace which lasted for three years was declared between the Dutch and the Swedes.

In endeavoring to understand the relations between the settlements of the different nations in America in the seventeenth century we must realize that the colonies were only pawns in the great game being played in Europe between Spain and the Papacy on the one hand and the Protestant countries, England, Sweden, and the United Netherlands on the other. Once apprehending this, we can easily understand why the governor of each colony, though instructed to seize and hold every foot of land which could be occupied, was advised not to antagonize the other friendly nations and thus weaken the alliance against the common enemy. As the power of Spain declined, however, and the estimate of the value of the American colonies increased, the friction in the New World became more acute and the instructions from the home governments grew imperative.

Affairs then came to an open rupture between New Netherland and New Sweden. In 1651 Governor Stuyvesant inaugurated a more aggressive policy against the Swedes by building Fort Casimir near what is now New Castle, Delaware, not far from the Swedish fort. Three years later Fort Casimir fell into the hands of the Swedes. The Dutch Government now commanded Stuyvesant to drive the Swedes from the river or compel their submission. As a result the Director and his fleet sailed into the Delaware in September, 1655, and captured one fort after another, till Rysing, the last of the Swedish governors, was completely defeated. Though the colonists were promised security in possession of their lands, the power of

New Sweden was ended, and the jurisdiction of the Dutch was for a time established.

New Netherland had, however, other neighbors more powerful, more persistent, and with more at stake than the French, the Indians, and the Swedes. These were the English colonists, pressing northward from the Virginias and southward from New England. From the beginning of the Dutch colonization, England had looked askance at the wedge thus driven between her own settlements. She had stubbornly refused to recognize the sovereignty of the States-General in the region of New Netherland while at the same time she vainly sought a pretext for the establishment of her own. England put forward the apocryphal claim of discovery by Cabot; but here she was stopped by the doctrine announced in a previous century that in order to give title to a new country, discovery must be followed by occupation. When England maintained that, since Hudson was an Englishman, the title to his discovery must pass to his native land, she was reminded that Cabot was a Genoese, and that Genoa might as well claim title to Virginia as England to New Netherland.

The Plymouth Company particularly was concerned at the Dutch occupation of this middle region to which the charter granted by King James gave it a claim. It formally protested in 1621 against these "Dutch intruders." Whereupon King James I directed Sir Dudley Carleton, his ambassador at The Hague, to protest against the Dutch settlements; but nothing was accomplished, both parties having their hands too full with European quarrels to carry these transatlantic matters to extremities. The tension, however, was constantly increased on both sides by a series of encroachments and provocations.

In April, 1633, for example, the ship *William* arrived at Fort Amsterdam under command of Captain Trevor, with Jacob Eelkens as supercargo. Eelkens had been dismissed by the West India Company from the post of Commissary at Fort Orange, and was now in the service of some London merchants, in whose behalf he had come, as he told the Director, to buy furs on Henry Hudson's River.

"Don't talk to me of Henry Hudson's River!" replied Van Twiller, "it is the River Mauritius." He then called for the commission of Eelkens, who refused to show it, saying that he was within the dominions of the English King, and a servant of His Majesty, and asking the Dutch Council what commission they themselves had to plant in the English dominion. Whereupon Van Twiller replied that it was not fitting that Eelkens should proceed up the river, as the whole of that country belonged to the Prince of Orange and not to the King of England.

After this exchange of amenities, Eelkens returned to his ship, which remained at anchor for several days. At the end of the time, he presented himself again at the fort to ask if the Director would consent in a friendly way to his going up the river; otherwise, he would proceed if it cost his life. In reply, Van Twiller ordered the Dutch flag to be run up at the fort and three pieces of ordnance fired in honor of the Prince of Orange. Eelkens on his part ordered the English flag to be hoisted on the *William* and a salute fired in honor of King Charles. Van Twiller warned Eelkens that the course which he was pursuing might cost him his neck; but the supercargo weighed anchor and proceeded calmly on his way.

Van Twiller then assembled all his forces before his door, brought out a cask of wine, filled a bumper, and cried out that those who loved the Prince of Orange and him should follow his example and protect him from the outrages of the Englishman;

Eelkens, by this time, was out of sight sailing up the river. The people drank, but only laughed at their governor, and De Vries told him that he had been very foolish. "If it were my affair," he said, "I would have helped him away from the fort with beans from the eight-pounders."

The *William*, meanwhile, journeyed up the river and Eelkens, who knew the country well, landed with his crew about a mile below Fort Orange and set up a tent where he displayed the wares which he hoped to exchange with the natives for beaver-skins. Very soon reports of this exploit reached the ears of the commissary at Fort Orange, who at once embarked with a trumpeter on a shallop decorated with green boughs. The Dutch landed close beside the English and set up a rival tent; but the Indians preferred to deal with Eelkens, whom they had known years before and who spoke their language.

In the high tide of success, however, Eelkens was rudely ordered to depart by a Dutch officer who had come up the river in charge of three vessels, a pinnace, a caravel, and a hoy. To enforce the commands came soldiery from both Dutch forts, armed with muskets, half-pikes, swords, and other weapons, and ordered Eelkens to strike his flag. They pulled down the tent, sent the goods on board ship, and sounded their trumpets in the boat "in disgrace of the English." The Dutch boarded the *William*, weighed her anchor, and convoyed her down the river with their fleet, and finally dismissed her at the mouth of the river.

The troubles of the Dutch with their English neighbors, however, did not end with these aggressions on the Hudson and similar acts on the Delaware. In the year 1614, Adriaen Block, a great navigator whose name deserves to rank with that of Hudson, had sailed through the East River, and putting boldly across Long Island Sound, had discovered the Housatonic and Connecticut rivers. He also discovered and gave his own name to Block Island and explored Narragansett Bay, whence he took his course to Cape Cod. These discoveries reported to the States-General of the United Netherlands caused their High Mightinesses at once to lay claim to the new lands; but before they could secure enough colonists to occupy the country, restless pioneers of English stock planted towns in the Connecticut valley, along the Sound, and on the shore of Long Island. These were uncomfortable neighbors with aggressive manners which quite upset the placid Dutch of New Amsterdam. Inevitable boundary disputes followed, which reached no adjustment until, in 1650, Stuyvesant went to Hartford to engage in a conference with commissioners of the United Colonies of New England.

The Director began as usual with bravado; but presently he consented to leave the question of boundaries to a board of four arbitrators. This board decided that the boundary between the Dutch and English possessions should run on Long Island from Oyster Bay south to the Atlantic, and that on the mainland it should run north from Greenwich Bay, but never approach within ten miles of the Hudson River. The Dutch in New Netherland were amazed and disgusted at the decision; but though Stuyvesant is said to have exclaimed in dramatic fashion that he had been betrayed, he found it hopeless to struggle against the superior force arrayed against him.

CHAPTER VIII

THE English Government was fortunate in its first representative after the surrender of Stuyvesant. Colonel Richard Nicolls, who had enforced the surrender with all the energy of a soldier, afterward displayed all the tact and wisdom of a statesman. It is true that the towns and forts were rechristened, and New Amsterdam, Fort Amsterdam, and Fort Orange became respectively New York, Fort James, and Albany in honor of the King's brother, James, Duke of York and Albany, to whom as Lord Proprietor the new English province was now granted; but the Dutch were not interfered with in their homes, their holdings, or their religion, and for nearly a year the city government at New Amsterdam went on as of old under the control of burgomasters, *schepens*, and *schouts*.

In the following year Nicolls, according to instructions from the Duke of York, abolished "the form of government late in practice," appointed a mayor, aldermen, and a sheriff to rule New York, and directed the new officials to swear allegiance to the Duke He continued the commercial rights of the freeman who represented the burghers of the Dutch period, and he also introduced trial by jury, which placated the dwellers at New York and along the Hudson.

On Long Island and in Westchester where New Englanders had settled, Nicolls proceeded with greater vigor. This section together with Staten Island was erected into the district of Yorkshire, where "the Duke's Laws" were proclaimed and the machinery of English county government was put in operation. With its three ridings, its courts of sessions, and its court of assizes, Yorkshire soon had an unmistakable English character even though Dutch inhabitants were numerous in western Long Island and in Staten Island. The Duke's Laws were compiled mainly from the laws of the New England colonies, though they departed in many particulars from New England traditions. In the Dutch towns *schouts* and *schepens* gave place to overseers and constables. The characteristic form of town government in the province was that in which freeholders elected a board of eight overseers and a constable for one year. Little by little English law and English institutions were to crowd out Dutch law and Dutch political institutions in the conquered province.

By his wise policy, his magnetic personality, his scholarly tastes, and his social geniality, Nicolls seems to have won all hearts. Maverick, his colleague, wrote Lord Arlington that it was wonderful how this man could harmonize things in a world so full of strife. Entrusted by the Duke of York with practically unlimited power, he used it with the utmost discretion and for the good of the province. When he resigned his post after four years of service, New York was deeply regretful over his departure and Cornelis Steenwyck, the Dutch mayor of the city, gave a farewell banquet in his honor.

His successor, Colonel Francis Lovelace, was a favorite at court and a gallant cavalier who had been loyal to the King throughout his adversity. With far less ability than Nicolls, Lovelace was at one with him in desire to benefit and unify the colony. He established a club where English, French, and Dutch were spoken, and he offered prizes to be run for on the Long Island race-course. Under his rule shipping increased and trade flourished. Merchants began to hold weekly meetings, thus laying the foundations of The Merchants' Exchange. But his most notable achievement was the establishment of the first mail service on the American continent.

In spite of all the sea commerce and trading up and down the river by sloops, pinks, flyboats, ketches, and canoes, the colonies of New York and New England demanded swifter and more frequent means of communication, and Governor Lovelace began to consider how the bonds could be drawn closer. In 1671 one John Archer bought part of Van der Donck's old estate and built a village "near unto the passage commonly called Spiting Devil" on "the road for passengers to go to and fro from the main as well as for mutual intercourse with the neighboring colony." Lovelace consented to make the village an enfranchised town by the name of Fordham Manor, provided its inhabitants should forward to the next town all public packets and letters coming to or going from New York. The scheme evidently proved a success, for Lovelace shortly decided on a wider extension of communication, and the year 1673 was celebrated by the setting out of the first post between New York and New England. It was to have started on New

Year's Day, but was delayed by waiting for news from Albany. On the arrival of communications from Albany the carrier was sworn into office, instructed "to behave civily," to inquire of the New England authorities as to the best post-road, and to mark it for the benefit of other travelers. The message which Lovelace sent to Governor Winthrop of Massachusetts on this occasion ran as follows:

I here present you with two rarities, a pacquett of the latest intelligence I could meet withal, and a Post. By the first, you will see what has been acted on the stage of Europe; by the latter you will meet with a monthly fresh supply; so that if it receive but the same ardent inclinations from you as at first it hath from myself, by our monthly advises all publique occurrences may be transmitted between us, together with severall other great conveniencys of publique importance, consonant to the commands laid upon us by His sacred Majestie, who strictly injoins all his American subjects to enter into a close correspondency with each other. This I look upon as the most compendious means to beget a mutual understanding; and that it may receive all the countenance from you for its future duration, I shall acquaint you with the model I have proposed; and if you please but to make an addition to it, or subtraction, or any other alteration, I shall be ready to comply with you. This person that has undertaken the imployment I conceaved most proper, being both active, stout, and indefatigable. He is sworne as to his fidelity. I have affixt an annuall sallery on him, which, together with the advantage of his letters and other small portable packes, may afford him a handsome livelyhood. Hartford is the first stage I have designed him to change his horse, where constantly I expect he should have a fresh one lye. All the letters outward shall be delivered gratis with a signification of *Post Payd* on the superscription; and reciprocally, we expect all to us free. Each first Monday of the month he sets out from New York, and is to return within the month from Boston to us againe. The maile has divers baggs, according to the townes the letters are designed to, which are all sealed up till their arrivement, with the seale of the Secretarie's Office, whose care it is on Saturday night to seale them up. Only by-letters are in an open bag, to dispense by the wayes. Thus you see the scheme I have drawne to promote a happy correspondence. I shall only beg of you your furtherance to so universall a good work.

By trail, road, and waterway the colonists were thus drawing nearer to each other and steadily increasing their facilities for trade, when all was interrupted by the reassertion of Dutch sovereignty and the reconquest of the English colony by the Dutch under much the same circumstances as had marked the surrender of Stuyvesant in 1664. The old habit of unpreparedness survived under the English as under the Dutch; and the third war between England and Holland, begun in 1672 and ended in 1674, found the strategic points on the Hudson again unprotected.   One August day in 1673 a powerful Dutch fleet appeared off Staten Island.   On the next day it sailed up through the Narrows, and Manhattan saw a repetition, with a difference, of the scene of 1664.   After a brief exchange of volleys between the strong fleet and the weak fortress, the garrison recognized that resistance was hopeless, New York surrendered to Admiral Evertsen, and the flag of the Dutch Republic floated once more over the fortress, which changed its name to Fort Willem Hendrick while New York became New Orange.   Governor Lovelace was absent from the city at the moment, and the blame of the surrender fell upon Manning, a subordinate, who was tried for neglect of duty, cowardice, and treachery.   His sword was broken over his head and he was pronounced ineligible for any office of trust.   But no governor could have saved the situation, as nothing was ready for defense.   When the Dutch took possession, Captain Anthony Colve was appointed Governor.   He proceeded with energy to put the fort into condition for defense, and for a time it seemed as if the Dutch might at last hold their rich heritage along the Hudson.   At the close of hostilities, however, a treaty which was signed at Westminster in February, 1674, and proclaimed at the City Hall of New Orange in July of the same year, stipulated that New Netherland should again become an English province. Thus for the third time, a national flag was lowered at the fort on Manhattan Island without serious effort at opposition.

The treaty did not restore New York to the Duke whose name it bore but handed it over directly to Charles II, who, however, again granted it to his brother James. Edmund Andros, a major in Prince Rupert's regiment of dragoons, was sent out to take control of the province, which had now changed hands for the last time. His character was probably neither so white nor so black as it has been painted; but it is certain that he lacked the tact of Nicolls, and he brought to his task the habits of a soldier rather than an administrator. He never succeeded in winning the complete confidence of the people.

From the beginning Andros showed himself hostile to popular liberty and loyal to the interests of his patron as he saw them. But the difficulties of his position, it must be admitted, were very great. James, Duke of York, brother of Charles II, and, in the absence of legitimate children of the King, the heir to the throne, had, as we have seen, been granted all rights in the conquered territory of New Netherland in 1664. Part of this territory he promptly gave to two court favorites, Lord Berkeley and Sir George Carteret. The sagacious Nicolls protested that this partition which surrendered to a divided ownership the rich lands of New Jersey — so called in honor of Carteret's gallant defense of the Island of Jersey during the Civil Wars — was a menace to the well-being of New York. His warning, which might not have been heeded in any case, did not reach England until the transfer was completed.

With the Dutch occupation all titles were canceled, but under the new treaty, James, although by this time thoroughly informed of the complications involved, with the usual fatuity of the Stuarts now made a grant of the eastern part of New Jersey to Carteret in severalty, taking no notice of the western part, which Berkeley had already sold for the sum of a thousand pounds. By this grant to Carteret many questions were at once raised. Was Sir George Carteret a lord proprietor like the Duke himself, responsible only to the King, or was he only a lord of the manor responsible to his master the Duke? Was East Jersey a part of New York, or was it an independent province? As usual the importance of the questions was based on commercial considerations. If New Jersey were a separate entity then it might trade directly with England; if it were dependent on New York it could trade only by permission of the Duke's representative.

Philip Carteret, a kinsman of Sir George, whom the latter had appointed Governor of his share of New Jersey, and who went to America in the same ship as Andros in 1674, determined to test the matter by declaring Elizabethtown a free port, while Andros demanded that all ships bound to or from any port in the original New Netherland must enter and clear at New York. With equal pertinacity Andros asserted the Duke's authority in West Jersey, haling Fenwick, one of the claimants under the original grant of 1674, to court in New York. Fenwick's land titles, however, were sustained, and Andros then released him upon his explicit promise that he would not meddle with the government of West Jersey. Taking advantage of the death of Sir George Carteret in 1680, Andros next arrested and imprisoned Governor Philip Carteret on the ground that he now had no authority, and then himself assumed the governorship of East Jersey. But Carteret was acquitted, the Assembly of East Jersey sustained their Governor, and the towns refused to submit. Meanwhile, charges of corruption had been brought against Andros in New York, where his imperious manner and arbitrary conduct had made enemies. He was recalled to England in 1681 to answer these charges, and in consequence of the disaffection which he had stirred up he was removed from office.

Colonel Thomas Dongan, the Governor chosen to succeed Andros, was a younger son of an Irish Baronet and a Roman Catholic. The laws of England forbade a Catholic to hold office in that country; but there was not the same barrier in the province subject to a Lord Proprietor. James, being of the Catholic faith, was therefore glad to appoint people of that religion in the New World. Realizing, however, that the feeling against Catholicism was strong in the colony, the Duke gilded the pill by granting more liberal laws and a more popular form of government than had previously been permitted. At the time of his appointment Dongan received instructions from the Duke of York to call a representative Assembly of not more than eighteen members to be chosen by the freeholders of the province. This Assembly met in October, 1683, and passed some fifteen laws, the first and most memorable of which was the so-called *Charter of Liberties and Privileges*. The most notable provisions of the charter were those establishing the principles of popular representation and religious liberty, and those reciting the guarantees of civil rights familiar to all Englishmen.

Before this charter could be finally ratified by the Duke of York, Charles II died from a stroke of apoplexy, and James became King. After fifteen minutes in his closet, where he had retired to give "full scope to his tears," he emerged to work for three years his bigoted will on the affairs of the realm. James the King took a different view of many things from James the Duke. The status of New York was similarly changed from a ducal proprietorship to a royal province. The new charter recognized a Lord Proprietor. But that Lord Proprietor had now become King of England, and this King found some of the enactments of the charter so objectionable to His Majesty that he disallowed the charter. Moreover, James did away with the Assembly which he had previously allowed to be summoned. But the seed of popular government had been planted in the Western

Hemisphere and within the next century it was ripe for the harvesting.

In 1688 New York and New Jersey were united with the Eastern colonies under title of " The Dominion of New England," and Sir Edmund Andros was appointed Governor-General of a territory of imperial dimensions. But the year of his arrival in New York marked the departure of his royal master from England. Bigotry and tyranny had overshot the mark and the English people had determined to dethrone James.

On the invitation of the Protestant nobility, James's son-in-law, William of Orange, landed at Torbay in November, 1688, and rapidly won popular support. After beginning negotiations with him, James became alarmed and took flight to France at the close of the year. William of Orange and his wife, James's daughter Mary, then became King and Queen of England (February 13, 1689) and New York once more passed under the control of a Dutch sovereign.

CHAPTER IX

THE story of the so-called Leisler Rebellion illustrates the difficulty of sifting conflicting historical testimony. Among the earlier chroniclers of New Netherland there is the widest difference of opinion about the chief actor in the drama. Leisler was "an illiterate German," says one authority. Another says: "He was the son of a French clergyman driven into exile, and making his home in Frankfort where the little Jacob was born. The boy was taught to write and speak Dutch, French, and German; but being unskilled in the English tongue he was unjustly charged with illiteracy." By one party he was branded as a vulgar demagogue ready to ally himself with the mob against the conservative citizenry. By another he was acclaimed as the champion of the people's rights and religion when they were threatened with invasion by the minions of the perfidious Stuarts.

In regard to the main events of this troubled time there is, fortunately, little dispute, although they are so complicated that they require close attention. When James II fled from England at the end of the year 1688 and was succeeded by William and Mary, the affairs of the American provinces were thrown into a state of chaos. The change of government was not known in Massachusetts until March, 1689. The immediate result of the news was to fan the popular wrath against Sir Edmund Andros, then in Boston, into such a flame that the Governor was seized and thrown into prison before he was able to make his escape to New York. His imprisonment left Lieutenant-Governor Nicholson, Andros's deputy at New York, in a difficult position. Andros was still Governor and Nicholson was unable to communicate with him. Some people held that Nicholson thus became acting Governor; others claimed that the whole existing machinery of government was swept away by the abdication of James and that the provinces were free to govern themselves till they could learn the will of the new sovereigns.

Nicholson was a weak man, and his vacillation produced the impression that he might be engaged in a conspiracy to bring back the rule of James.

Three years before, in the King's camp, he had
knelt when Mass was celebrated. Who knew what
Catholic designs might lurk behind this significant
act? Rumor grew into suspicion, and suspicion
turned to panic. At length Nicholson fell into an
altercation with an officer on guard at Fort James
who asserted his authority. In the course of
the argument the Lieutenant-Governor remarked
angrily: "I would rather see the city on fire
than commanded by an impudent fellow like
him." Next morning word had spread far and wide
through the town that Nicholson had threatened
to burn New York, and all was in an uproar. A
crowd of citizens appeared at the house of Leisler
who was an officer in the train-band, a citizen well
known for honesty, a stanch, even bigoted Protestant, and withal a man of firm purpose, and
they begged him to act as their leader in a determined effort to preserve their liberties and hold
New York for William and Mary. It is easy to
see on looking back over two centuries that the
dangers of conspiracy were greatly exaggerated
but we must remember that these men really
believed that they themselves and all that they
held sacred were in jeopardy. The possibility of
war with France was indeed not remote; and fear

of an invasion from Canada with all the horrors of an Indian war haunted the minds of every frontier family.

Leisler invited the people of the towns and counties of New York to choose delegates to a convention to be held at Fort James on June 25, 1689, to consider what was best to be done under existing conditions. Ulster, Albany, and most of the towns in Queens County refused to send delegates. The others responded, however, and the delegates formed themselves into a committee of safety. They appointed Leisler "Captain of the fort at New York until orders shall be received from their Majesties," and Leisler accepted the responsibilities of government.

Massachusetts and Connecticut congratulated him on his conduct, and in the province of New York he was generally approved; but he had the misfortune to be opposed by the Roman Catholics and the landed gentry. The former were few in number and, after the establishment of the Protestant succession, a negligible danger, though in view of the assertion made by James to the Pope that "it was his full purpose to have set up Roman Catholic Religion in the English Plantations of America," we can scarcely call it bigotry on

Leisler's part to fear their influence. Unfortunately for the Leislerians "the gentry" made common cause with the Catholics against the new Government. Albany, which was preëminently Dutch and held the Reformed Church in reverence, was also aristocratic in sympathy and resented the rule of Leisler as the representative of the common people. Even so, had Leisler shown more tact and less obstinacy there might still have been a chance to placate the opposing factions; but by his fanatical attacks on all Catholics and his open defiance of such prominent citizens as Nicholas Bayard, Stephanus Van Cortlandt, Frederick Philipse, Peter Schuyler, and Robert Livingston, he fomented the strife until conciliation became impossible.

In the beginning of January, 1689, Leisler committed a grievous strategical error in permitting Nicholson to leave for England to render an account of the state of affairs, while the Leislerians depended upon communications written in dubious English and carried by a bearer who was of inferior social standing.

Meanwhile Leisler won a temporary victory over his opponents. In December dispatches arrived from the Privy Council and the King and Queen of England, addressed to "Our Lieutenant-Governor and Commander-in-Chief of our Province of New York, or in his absence to such as for the time being take care to keep the peace and administer the laws," and authorizing him to take the reins of government, calling to his assistance "in the administration thereof the principal freeholders and inhabitants of the same, or so many of them as you shall think fit." Nicholson having departed for England, the messenger was in some doubt as to the proper recipient of the message. Bayard and his faction strove to obtain possession of it; but it was finally delivered to Leisler. He appointed a council of eight men, all reputable citizens and by no means representing the rabble, as his enemies charged. In this procedure he was acting in strict conformity with the letter from the Privy Council.

Leisler assumed the title of Lieutenant-Governor and, much to the chagrin of his foes, took his seat in the Governor's pew at church. It was his moment of triumph; but troubles were already darkening the horizon. In November Leisler sent to Albany his deputy, an Englishman named Milborne, to demand the recognition of his Government; but the mandate being opposed by Schuyler, Livingston, and Bayard, all well known and highly

esteemed in Albany and representing the aristocratic faction, that town refused entrance to
Milborne and his escort and refused likewise to
recognize Leisler as Governor.

The Albany Records for November, 1689, describe the incident as follows: "Three sloops neared
Albany bearing troops under Jacob Milborne and
immediately Captain Wendell and Blucker, Johannes Cuyler and Reymier Barents go aboard to
learn the object of his visit. Jacob Milborne asks:
'Is the fort open to receive me and my men?' The
reply is: 'No, the Mayor is in command and will
hold it.'"

On the receipt of this inhospitable message,
reënforced by military demonstrations, Milborne
wisely withdrew his inadequate force and returned
to New York to report the failure of his mission.
Three months after Milborne's rejection, in the
bitter February weather of 1690, the village of
Schenectady, at that time a western frontier post,
was burned and its inhabitants were massacred in
a French and Indian raid. Once more Leisler sent
his deputy at the head of a body of troops to the
assistance of the Albanians, and this time Milborne
was not denied entrance to the town. Having thus
gained control of the province, Leisler summoned

a convention of delegates from Massachusetts and Connecticut to meet at New York on May 1, 1690, in order to discuss the defense of the colonies.

Meanwhile the Leislerians and their opponents were bombarding the new King and Queen with their conflicting claims. In 1690, Captain Blagge, congratulating their Majesties on "the late Happy Revolution in England" asked their Majesties' approbation for Leisler on the ground that "Nicholson, like Col. Dongan, had neglected to repair the fortifications of the city, which excited suspicions against his loyalty, and he was disaffected towards the late happy revolution in England." Hence Jacob Leisler had been chosen, "with a committee, to make such repairs and to administer the government until William's pleasure could be known." The memorial goes on to say:

Shortly after, their Majesties' Proclamation arrived by which William and Mary were to be proclaimed King and Queen of England. Notice was given to the late Council of Nicholson, and to the Mayor and Aldermen to assist, with proper ceremonies, in this Proclamation. They desired an hour's time for considering it, and then refused. Leisler and his Committee and most of the inhabitants did then celebrate the event with many demonstrations of joy and affection.

The Mayor and Aldermen were then suspended from

office, and certain opponents of the Revolution and their Majesties' interests, were imprisoned. Shortly after their Majesties' letters arrived, directed to Lieutenant Governor Nicholson, or, "in his absence to such as for the time being do take care for the preservation of their Majesties' Peace, and administering the Lawes in that their Majesties' Province; ordering such to take upon them the place of Lieutenant Governor and Commander in Chief of the said Province and to proclaim King William and Queen Mary, King and Queen of England, Scotland, France and Ireland, and supream Lord and Lady of the Province of New York, if not already done" which was accordingly done.

The Inhabitants generally were satisfied therewith and Leisler's committee was dismissed, and a Council chosen to assist him in the government; but the members of the old government opposed all this and created a faction. This excited fear lest the Province should yet be delivered up to the French in Canada, which fear greatly agitated the Protestant population. The said faction also surrounded Captain Leisler and abused him with ill language and threats, and would have done violence to him, if they had not feared the people, who rescued him out of their hands, and imprisoned the ringleaders of the opposition. Multitudes also flocked into the city from the country, to defend the existing government, and it was with great difficulty that their zeal could be restrained. The prisoners were ultimately fined and discharged upon their own recognizance to keep the peace.

The Fort and City were therefore, now in a good condition, excepting a lack of ammunition. The Commission of all military men who had acted under Governor

Dongan and Andros, had been called in, and other
Commissions issued in the name of their present Majesties, and only to those who were well affected thereto.
But our efforts thus to secure their Majesties interests
have been greatly misrepresented, and we have been
loaded with reproaches; our actions have been called a
Dutch plot, although three quarters of the inhabitants
are of Dutch descent, and speak Dutch; and our ruin is
threatened, if the government ever falls into the hands
of our opponents.

To this lengthy defense Bayard and Nicolls
made response as follows:

Jacob Leisler a man of desperate fortune, ambitiously
did assume unto himselfe the title of Lieutenant-Governor of this Province of New York, and chose a councel of
ye meanest and most abject common people; made to
himself a Broad Seale, which he called ye Seale of ye
Province, with ye usuall armes of Kings of England;
and affixed the same to some unlawful graunts of land
within this Province; and commissionated under ye
same Justices of ye Peace, in whose hartes were mis-
chiefe. He constituted Courts of Oyer and Terminer,
and tryed severall subjects for pretended treason,
murther and other crimes. He taxed and levied monney
upon their Majesties subjects to their grievous oppres-
sion and great impoverishment. When he wanted more
money for his occasions, he forcebly robbed and spoiled,
broke open doors and locx were he guissed it was to be
found, and carried away to ye vallue of some thousands
of pounds in money or goods; and all this against the

best Protestant subjects in the Province. He imprisoned whom he feared, without any other cause than that their integrity to ye Protestant interest, and fidelity to their Majesties, became a terroire to him; some of them after a tedious confignment, without collour of law, he whipt and branded; and some he kept in duresse so long as he held ye fort.

Upon one point, both the followers and opponents of Leisler agreed: there was no Dutch plot behind this revolution. "The notion of a Dutch plott cannot be applicable to Leisler and his adherents," said Bayard; "the much greater part of Albany which wholly consists of Dutch people, and all the men of best repute for religion, estatte, and integrity of the Dutch nacon, throughout the whole Province, having alwaies been manifestly against Leisler and his society, in all their illegall and irregular proceedings." To these representations their Majesties' advisers made no reply, but the appointment of Governor of New York was given to Colonel Henry Sloughter, "a profligate, needy, and narrow minded adventurer," the selection of whom did little credit to the wisdom of William of Orange. All the papers from both factions were committed to this inefficient officer with instructions to examine the allegations strictly and impartially and to make a true report.

In December, 1690, Sloughter set sail with several ships and a body of troops. By some accident the vessels were separated, and the ship bearing Major Richard Ingoldesby, "a rash, hot-headed man" who had served in Holland and recently returned from service in Ireland, arrived in the *Beaver* two months before Sloughter's ship reached New York. His commission required him to obey the royal Governor, but did not give him authority to act as commander-in-chief in case of Sloughter's absence or death. Nevertheless Ingoldesby at once announced the appointment of Sloughter and demanded the surrender of the fort. Leisler replied by offering quarters for Ingoldesby's soldiers; but refused to surrender the fort till he saw the Major's commission.

Ingoldesby had no credentials whatever, but he issued a proclamation calling on the people and magistrates to aid him in enforcing the royal commission. Leisler issued a counter proclamation warning him at his peril not to attempt hostilities against the city or the fort; but on receiving assurances that Ingoldesby had no intention of using force against the people of New York, he permitted the troops to land. The fort, however, he would not yield. With rival forces in the town, peace was difficult to maintain. Neither commander trusted the other. Recrimination followed protest. Finally, on the 17th of March, Leisler fired on Ingoldesby's troops, killing two and wounding others.

At length on March 19, 1691, Sloughter entered the harbor of New York. Representative anti-Leislerians hastened to board his ship and escorted him to the City Hall, where he took the oath of office at eleven o'clock at night. He immediately dispatched Ingoldesby to demand the surrender of the fort. Again Leisler's bigotry and obstinacy overcame his prudence. Instead of surrendering at once he dispatched a messenger bearing letters and warning him to look well at Sloughter and be sure he was no counterfeit. Sloughter informed Leisler's messenger that he intended to make himself known in New York as well as in England and ordered Ingoldesby for the second time to demand possession of the fort and to release from their prison Colonel Bayard and Mr. Nicolls, that they might attend the council to which they had been appointed members.

Leisler refused either to surrender the fort or to release the prisoners but sent Milborne and De la Noy to endeavor to make terms. Sloughter imprisoned both envoys and ordered his frigate to hold itself in readiness to fire on the fort. Leisler, at length and too late realizing that resistance was useless, sent a letter to the Governor offering submission. For the third time Ingoldesby was ordered to demand the possession of the fort. This time the garrison yielded and Leisler was put under arrest.

With Milborne, now his son-in-law, and eight others, Leisler was arraigned before a court having inveterate royalists as judges. Two insurgents were acquitted. Six made their defense, were convicted of high treason, and were reprieved. Leisler and Milborne declined to plead and appealed to the King. They were, however, condemned and sentenced to death. Sloughter was reluctant to sign the death-warrants; but his associates, more particularly Bayard, who had been imprisoned by Leisler, were determined on the execution. It is maintained that the Governor's signature was obtained at a banquet when he was under the influence of liquor, and that an officer stole with the warrant to the prison and ordered the victims led out for immediate execution. Be this as it may, Sloughter's compunctions were overcome and the death-warrants signed.

The scaffold was erected at the lower end of the park and weeping people thronged about the victims. Leisler's dying speech, which was marked by neither anger nor bitterness, affirmed that he had no other aim than "to maintain against Popery or any schism or heresy whatever the interest of our Sovereign Lord and Lady and the Reformed Protestant Churches" in these parts. The drop fell, the populace rushed up to claim some relics of their leader, the bodies were taken down, beheaded, and buried, and so the worthless Sloughter thought to make an end of "a troublesome fellow."

But the Leisler blood still flowed in the veins of the dead man's son, who never ceased fighting till in 1695 the attainder on the estate was removed. This action of the English Parliament was tantamount to a confession that Leisler had been unjustly accused, tried, and hanged, and that these, the only people ever put to death for political reasons on the soil of New York, died as misguided martyrs, not as criminal conspirators.

CHAPTER X

SLOUGHTER did not live long to enjoy his triumph over Leisler, and his death came so suddenly that the anti-Leislerites raised their eyebrows and whispered "poison," while the Leislerites shrugged their shoulders and sneered "delirium tremens." Neither faction seemed particularly reluctant to part with him.

Colonel Benjamin Fletcher, who was sent over from England as the next Governor, arrived in New York in the summer of 1692. His rule is chiefly memorable for the founding of Trinity Church and for the encouragement which he gave to piracy. These strangely differing activities were both obnoxious to the Dutch burghers, who were almost as strongly opposed to the Church of England as to that of Rome, and who suspected the Governor of conniving at the practice of piracy or at least of closing his eyes to the source of the doubloons of Spain, the louis d'or of France, and other strange coin which at this epoch had begun to circulate together with ivory and sandalwood in the little town at the tip of Manhattan Island.

In one sense Fletcher cannot be held responsible for the existence of piracy in the colony or on the high seas. The institution was as old as navigation. Moreover the issuance of letters of marque in the war with Spain had legalized privateering, which was so near akin to piracy that it was often hard to distinguish between the two. Even royalty was not above accepting a share in the questionable spoils of the sea, as in the well-known case of Queen Elizabeth and the booty which Drake brought home.

It is easy, therefore, to guess the source of the Eastern rugs, the carved teakwood furniture, and stuffs from India looms which adorned the houses of the rich men of New York. On the streets pirate captains were pointed out as celebrities. One of them, Edward Coates, presented Madam Fletcher with jewels, silks, and cashmere shawls. Thomas Tew, another "filibustier," is described by a contemporary as a slight, dark man about forty years of age, who wore a uniform consisting of a blue jacket bordered with gold lace and short trousers of white linen covering his legs to the knee, below which came embroidered stockings. Around his neck he wore a chain of beaten gold and from his belt protruded a dagger's hilt set with sparkling jewels.

These picturesque pirates and privateers swaggered about the taverns in the shadow of the *Stadt-Huys* or lounged along the wharves at the harbor. Everywhere they were the center of attention, and their tales of adventure were listened to with the most eager interest. But these adventurers in the end pushed things so far that the Government in England found itself obliged to take vigorous action against them. James expressly instructed the provincial Governors Andros and Dongan to suppress "all pirates and sea rovers," for they had become so bold in their activities along the Spanish Main that lawful trading was languishing and merchants were in terror.

Many of the adventurers in the West Indies having been originally engaged in the honest business of *boucanning*, or smoking fish and meat after the manner of the Carib savages, they and their piratical comrades were generally known in Europe as "buchaniers" or "buccaneers." By the Hollanders they were named "*zee rovers*"; by the

French "*flibustiers*," which was only the French-man's way of pronouncing "freebooter." In 1652 Samuel Sewall established in Boston a free mint, which attracted the pirates to that town, where they could bring their booty in gold and silver and have it safely dropped into the melting-pot beyond the reach of either discovery or recovery. In 1687 Sir Robert Holmes was sent with a squadron to the West Indies to put a stop to the nefarious trade of the freebooters, and in the next year Nicholson imprisoned at Boston several pirates whose leader was "one Petersen." These activities on the part of the authorities had the effect of driving the "*zee rovers*" from the Caribbean to the East Indies for their enterprises and from Boston to New York for their market.

Sea commerce at this time had so far outstripped a naval power adequate to protect it that piracy grew more and more profitable, and many a respected merchant held private stock in some more than dubious sea venture. The coast of Madagascar was a meeting place for pirates and merchantmen, and there Oriental stuffs, gold, and jewels were exchanged for rum or firearms, and the merchant vessel returned to New York, where her goods were sold cheaply and no questions were asked. One ship sailing from New York laden with Jamaica rum, Madeira wine, and gunpowder returned with a cargo of slaves and East India goods, and the voyage was reported to have cleared a net profit of thirty thousand pounds.

The scandal of "adventuring" continued to grow, and in 1695 Peter De la Noy wrote thus to the home government:

We have a parcell of pirates in these parts which (people) call the Red Sea men, who often get great booty of Arabian Gold. His Excellency gives all due encouragement to these men, because they make all due acknowledgements to him; one Coats, a captain of this honorable order presented his Excellency with his ship, which his Excellency sold for eight hundred pounds and every one of the crew made him a suitable present of Arabian Gold for his protection; one Captain Twoo who is gone to the Red Sea upon the same errand was before his departure highly caressed by His Excellency in his coach and six horses, and presented with a gold watch to engage him to make New York his port at his return. Twoo retaliated the kindnesse with a present of jewells; but I can't learn how much further the bargain proceeded; time must shew that. . . . After this all you will perhaps wonder when I tell you that this man's bell rings twice a day for prayers and that he appears with a great affectation of piety; but this is true, and it is as true that it makes him only more ridiculous, not more respected.

Not only were the buccaneers terrorizing the West Indies, the Red Sea, and the Madagascar coast, but according to the Albany Records of 1696 "pirates in great numbers infest the Hudson River at its mouth and waylay vessels on their way to Albany, speeding out from covers and from behind islands and again returning to the rocky shores, or ascending the mountains along the river to conceal their plunder."

The Government in England now prepared to take vigorous measures. It desired to fit out an armed force to suppress the buccaneers; but as all the regular navy was needed in the war with France it was decided to organize a stock company in which the King, the Duke of Shrewsbury, Lord Chancellor Somers, the Earls of Bellomont, Orford, and Romney, Robert Livingston, and others took shares, for the purpose of fitting out a privateer vessel to fight the pirates and at the same time to win some profit for themselves.

The *Adventure-Galley*, carrying thirty guns and manned by over one hundred sailors, was fitted out and entrusted to the command of William Kidd, a sea-captain of New York who chanced to be in London at the time and who was warmly recommended by Robert Livingston to Lord Bellomont, who had been appointed to succeed Fletcher as Governor of New York. He was well known as a bold and skillful sailor, and a man of wealth and repute in New York, and in his marriage certificate he was called "Captain William Kidd, Gentleman."

The plan finally formed was that Kidd with a privateer furnished with a letter of marque and a special commission from the King should cruise about in search of the pirates and capture them. In pursuance of the scheme Kidd set sail on the *Adventure-Galley* and reached New York in the spring of 1696. He set up placards all over the town asking for recruits, with the result that a motley crew of adventurers rushed to take ship in this strange new enterprise. At this time Kidd was living in one of the handsomest houses in New York, on what is now Liberty Street. Before this, in 1691, he had married the widow of a fellow sea-captain, a woman of great respectability, by whom he had one daughter, and he was known far and wide as a solid and trustworthy merchant.

His venture seemed bulwarked by every guarantee; but even at that epoch there were not wanting those who predicted strange things for the *Adventure-Galley*. Few, however, foresaw any events as strange as those which actually occurred. After

cruising along the American coast without achiev-
ing the capture of any pirate ships Kidd set sail for
the Red Sea and reached the coast of Madagascar
in the fall of 1697. Here again he found no trace
of the corsairs, who had probably been forewarned
of his coming.

Kidd then took on water and provisions and
proceeded to the coast of Madagascar. Still no
pirates. Water and provisions were running low,
and the crew threatened mutiny unless they were
allowed to take up the business of piracy on their
own account. Kidd thereupon decided to yield,
and the *Adventure-Galley* began by capturing several vessels owned by the Great Mogul, as well
as some ships sailing under French colors. In
December, 1698, Kidd captured an East India
ship named the *Quedagh Merchant*. The *Adventure-Galley* being in bad condition, Kidd set the
crew of the *Quedagh Merchant* on shore, took possession of the ship, burned his old one, and set sail
in his new vessel for Madagascar.

In spite of their rich spoils, the mutineers remained sullen, and many deserted. The men's
discontent led to an altercation with William
Moore, a gunner, in the course of which Kidd hit
him on the head with a bucket. The resulting

injury proved fatal to Moore and ultimately re-
sulted in disaster for Kidd.   After leaving Madagascar the pirate captain sailed for the West
Indies, and it must have been with a sinking heart
that he received the news which awaited him
there.   The piracy of the *Adventure-Galley* was
already known in England, and a committee of
Parliament had been appointed to inquire into
the whole affair.   Free pardon for acts committed
before May 1, 1699, was offered by royal proclamation to all pirates who would surrender.   But an
ominous exception was made in this proclamation of mercy: Avery, a notorious buccaneer, and
William Kidd were not included.

The cause of this exclusion from grace is not far
to seek.   It was not that Kidd was a sinner above
all others; but that he had involved great person-
ages from the King down, and that the Tories were
making capital out of the connection between
prominent Whig statesmen and the misdeeds of
Captain Kidd.   The outlaw now determined on
a course which in a righteous cause might well have
been called bold but which under the circumstances could only be described as brazen.   He
bought at the island of Hispaniola a small sloop
which he loaded with gold coin, gold dust, gems,

and other booty and, with what remained of his crew, he set sail for New York. Thus at San Domingo the *Quedagh Merchant*, with her fifty guns and her valuable cargo, was abandoned. Her fate has continued a mystery to this day, and from time to time the search for the lost booty is still suggested and inaugurated by enthusiasts for adventure or seekers for gold.

When Kidd drew near New York he found that the Earl of Bellomont had gone to Boston, and he resolved to follow the Governor to Massachusetts. Much uncertainty surrounds his course at this time. It is said that he sailed up Long Island Sound, stopped at Gardiner's Island, and buried a chest of treasure there, that he presented Mrs. Gardiner with brocades embroidered with gold threads and dropped jewels into his wine. It is said that he succeeded in reaching his wife by a letter, asking her to meet him at Block Island. Rumor has it that from Narragansett Bay he communicated with Bellomont and informed his lordship that he, William Kidd, was on board a sloop with ten thousand pounds' worth of goods and that he was entirely guiltless of the piracy with which he was charged. It is said that Bellomont replied that, if Kidd could establish his innocence, he might count on the Governor's protection.[1]

Amid all these rumors there seems good evidence that Kidd landed in Boston in July and had the effrontery to offer the Governor a gift of jewels for Lady Bellomont. With the approval of the Council Bellomont accepted the gift and handed the gems to a trustee as evidence in the case against Kidd. The Earl of Bellomont, being a man of sterling integrity, was naturally sensitive as to his apparent complicity in the Kidd piracy, refused any further parley, and sent the buccaneer to England to stand his trial there.

Kidd was held in London for several months pending the collection of evidence against him, and his trial for piracy and the murder of William Moore finally began at the Old Bailey in the spring of 1701. From this point we have the original documents of the state trials and a complete record of the evidence for and against Kidd. Bellomont is eliminated as a factor, and it becomes a case of the Crown against Captain William Kidd and a number of others, for murder and piracy upon the high seas.

[1] Bellomont was commissioned Governor of Massachusetts and New Hampshire, as well as of New York.

However we may feel as to Kidd's guilt in the matter of piracy, we can but realize that, according to the standards of modern times, he was not given a fighting chance for his life. He was detained in Newgate Prison and denied all counsel until he had pleaded "guilty" or "not guilty." In spite of all his protests he was brought to trial on the first indictment for murder, incidentally the least certain of his offenses. The jury being sworn, the clerk proceeded with the first indictment for murder and declared that "the jurors of our sovereign Lord the King do upon their oath present that William Kidd, late of London, married, not having the fear of God before his eyes; but being moved and seduced by the Devil . . . did make assault in and upon one William Moore . . . and that the aforesaid William Kidd with a certain wooden bucket, bound with iron hoops, of the value of eight pence, which he the said William Kidd then and there held in his right hand, did violently, feloniously, voluntarily, and of his malice aforethought beat and strike the aforesaid William Moore in and upon the right part of the head of him, the said William Moore then and there upon the high sea in the ship aforesaid and within the jurisdiction of England."

Several sailors testified to the circumstances of the murder, that Kidd had called the gunner "a lousy dog" and Moore had replied: "If I am a lousy dog you have made me so. You have brought me to ruin and many more." At this, Kidd's temper being roused, he struck Moore with the bucket, and the gunner died the next day as a result of the blow. Considering the severity of treatment of mutinous sailors permitted to ships' officers at that time, there is little reason to think that under ordinary circumstances Kidd would have been adjudged guilty of murder for a blow struck in hot blood and under provocation; but the verdict was certain before the trial had begun. The jury after an hour's consultation brought in a verdict of guilty, and Kidd was remanded to Newgate Prison to await trial for piracy.

This second trial took place in May, 1701, and included, beside the Captain, nine other mariners charged with piracy, in that "they feloniously did steal, take and carry away the said merchant ship *Quedagh Merchant* and the apparel and tackle of the same ship of the value of four hundred pounds of lawful money of England, seventy chests of opium, besides twenty bales of raw silk, a hundred bales of calico, two hundred bales of muslins, two hundred and fifty bales of sugar and three bales of romels."

Kidd's defense was that the ships captured were sailing under French passes and therefore lawful prizes according to the terms of his commission. These passes, he said, had been delivered into Bellomont's hands. But the Court made no effort to procure these passes or to inquire further into the matter. The jury was out for a short time only and brought in their verdict against or for the mariners separately. All but three were found guilty. In addressing them the Court said: "You have been tried by the laws of the land and convicted and nothing now remains but that sentence be passed according to the law. And the sentence of the law is this: You shall be taken from the place where you are and be carried to the place from whence you came and from thence to the place of execution and there be severally hanged by your necks until you be dead. And may the Lord have mercy on your souls!"

Captain Kidd was hanged at Execution Dock on May 23, 1701. Thus ended the most famous pirate of the age. His career so impressed the popular imagination that a host of legends sprang up concerning him and his treasure ship, while

innumerable doleful ballads were written setting
forth his incredible depravity.   Yet it is curious to
consider that, had he died a few years earlier, he
would have passed away as an honored citizen of
New York and would have been buried with pomp
and circumstance and the usual laudatory funeral
oration.

CHAPTER XI

WHILE Captain Kidd was still on the high seas and pirates were still infesting the lower Hudson, the Earl of Bellomont arrived in New York (in April, 1698), accompanied by his wife and his cousin, John Nanfan, who had been appointed Lieutenant-Governor. The citizens greeted the new Governor with every demonstration of delight. The corporation gave a public banquet and offered a eulogistic address. Bellomont on his part entered into his task with enthusiasm. In the new Assembly called in 1699, he spoke of the disorder prevailing in the province, left as it was with a divided people, an empty treasury, ruined fortifications, and a few half-naked soldiers. He spoke of the ill repute of New York as a rendezvous for pirates and said: "It would be hard if I who come before you with an honest heart and a resolution to be just to your interests, should meet with greater difficulties in the discharge of His Majesty's service than those who have gone before me." He declared it his firm intention that there should be no more misapplication of the public money, a veiled attack upon Fletcher's grants of land and privileges which had become a public scandal. He would, he said, pocket none of the money himself nor permit any embezzlement of it by others and promised exact accounts to be laid before the Assembly "when and as often as you require." The Assembly passed a vote of thanks and voted a six years' revenue. Apparently everything was auspicious; but the seed of discord was already sown by Bellomont's early espousal of the Leislerian cause, which was in effect the cause of the common people.

In the Ecclesiastical Records of the State an account of the disinterment and reburial of the mutilated remains of Leisler and of his son-in-law Milborne shows the determination of Bellomont to make what reparation was possible, in addition to the removal of attainder, for the injustice done. The document closes with these words:

Yesterday, October 20, [1698] the remains of Commander Jacob Leisler and of Jacob Milborne [eight years and

five months after their execution and burial] were ex-
humed, and interred again with great pomp under our
[new] Dutch Church [in Garden Street]. Their weapons
and armorial ensigns of honor were there [in the Church]
hung up, and thus, as far as it was possible, their honor
was restored to them. Special permission to do this
had been received by his Honor's son, Jacob Leisler,
from his Majesty. This gave unutterable joy to their
families and to those people who, under him, had taken
up arms for our blessed King William. With this circumstance we trust that the dissensions which have so
long harassed us, will also be buried. To this end our
Right Honorable Governor, my lord the Earl of Bellomont, long wished for by us, is exerting his good offices.
He tries to deal impartially with all, acting with great
fairness and moderation. He has begun [his adminis-
tration] by remembering the Lord God; for he has
ordered a day of solemn fasting and prayer throughout
the whole land. In a proclamation of great seriousness,
he has exhorted the inhabitants earnestly to pray for
these things [peace among the people] to the Divine
Majesty. We hope the Lord will bestow his gracious
blessings and grace, upon your Reverences, with all our
hearts.

This proceeding on the part of Bellomont, combined with the appointment to office of prominent
Leislerians and the dismissal of some of their
opponents, arrayed at once a formidable body of
important citizens against him. Their numbers
were augmented by the people who had profited by

unlawful privileges won from Fletcher and now stripped from them by Bellomont; but the Governor pursued his course undaunted either by the threats or by the taunts cast against him as a partner of the pirate, Captain Kidd. So beloved was Bellomont by the people and so strongly intrenched by influence in the Government at home that he could probably have carried through the reforms which he had at heart; but his untimely death in 1701, after a brief rule of three years, put an end to all his far-reaching schemes for the good of the colonies.

His death was followed by a condition approaching civil war between the followers of Leisler and their foes. In 1702 Queen Anne, who had recently ascended the throne, appointed as Governor her relative, Edward Hyde, Lord Cornbury. He suppressed the Leislerians and exalted the aristocratic party, thereby restoring order but at the same time bringing odium upon his cause by his personal vices. Cornbury was a type of everything that a colonial governor should not be, a scamp, a spendthrift, and a drunkard. Relying upon his relationship to Queen Anne, he felt himself superior to the ordinary restraints of civilization. He took bribes under guise of gifts, was addicted to all forms of debauchery, and incidentally proved as foolish as he was wicked, one of his amusements, it is said, being that of parading the streets of New York in the evening, clad in woman's attire   His lady was as unpopular as he and it is said that when the wheels of her coach were heard approaching the house of any of the wealthy citizens of New York, the family was hastily set to work hiding the attractive ornaments to which her ladyship might take a fancy, as she had no compunction in asking for them as a gift.   In an expedition to Albany in 1702, Cornbury's vanity led him to decorate his barge with brilliant colors, to provide new uniforms for the crew, and generally to play the peacock at the expense of the colony.   Rumor placed the sum of his debts at £7000.   Moreover he was charged with the embezzlement of £1500 of government money.

A long-suffering community finally demanded the recall of Lord Cornbury and demanded it with the same insistence which was to make itself felt in revolution in the last half of the century. As is usual with sovereigns when any right is demanded with sufficient firmness, Queen Anne was graciously pleased to withdraw Lord Cornbury in 1708.   On the arrival of his successor, Cornbury was placed by indignant creditors in the charge of the sheriff, and was held in custody until the news of his succession to the earldom of Clarendon reached the colony. The library, furniture, and pictures of the Queen's cousin were sold at auction, while the ex-Governor skulked back to England to make the best possible showing as to his appropriation of public moneys to private uses. We can picture him wiping his eyes in pathetic deprecation, as he exclaimed: "If the Queen is not pleased to pay me, the having the Government of New Jersey, which I am persuaded the Queen intended for my benefit, will prove my ruin!"

Lord Lovelace, Cornbury's successor, demanded a permanent revenue. But recent experience had taught the colonists to hold the financial power in their own hands and they consented only to an annual appropriation, thus making the salary of the Governor dependent on his good conduct. What would have been the result of this clash of interests will never be known, since Lord Lovelace died on May 5, 1709, the same day on which the act was passed.

Major Richard Ingoldesby, Leisler's old enemy, now came into power and held the reins for a few months, until mismanagement of an expedition against Canada caused such indignation that he was withdrawn and Robert Hunter became Governor in 1710. Although of humble Scotch parentage he had risen to prominence in English society, numbering Swift and Addison among his friends and being married to Lady Hay, whose influence had procured for him successive positions of importance which culminated in this appointment.

With a view to encouraging the production of naval stores and obtaining a profit for the English Government, Hunter brought over at the expense of the Crown several thousand Palatines, German inhabitants of the Rhine valley harried by the French, thereby adding another alien element to the cosmopolitan population. The British Government appropriated the sum of £10,000 for the project and agreed not only to transport the emigrants but to maintain them for a time in return for their labor. These Palatines settled on both banks of the Hudson in four villages on lands belonging to Robert Livingston, and in three on those belonging to the Crown and situated on the west side of the river.

Authorities differ so widely in respect to the treatment of these German immigrants that it seems only fair to present both sides. One shows

Hunter working in the interest of the English Government against that of the colony and represents the movement as a clever plan on the part of the Governor to stimulate the production of tar and turpentine, to contribute to the government income, and to prevent the manufacture of wool, linen, and cotton goods, which at that time were largely bought in England. When Hunter found that the income did not meet the outlay, it is said, he notified the newcomers that they "must shift for themselves but not outside the province."

On the other hand, the Governor asserted that dwellers in the lower Palatinate of the Rhine, when driven from their homes by the French, begged the English Government to give them homes in America; that Queen Anne graciously agreed that the Palatines should be transported to New York at the expense of the English with the understanding that they were to work out the advance payment and also the food and lodgings provided by the State and by Livingston; but that the Palatines proved lazy and failed to carry out their contract.

All accounts agree, however, in describing the hard lot of these unfortunate exiles. Their ocean voyage was long and stormy with much fatal illness. The sites selected for their settlements were not desirable. The native pine was found unsuited to the production of tar in large quantities. They soon discovered that they would never be able to pay for their maintenance by such unprofitable labor. Moreover, the provisions given them were of inferior quality; and they were forced to furnish men for an expedition against Canada while their women and children were left either to starvation or to practical servitude. In this desperate situation some of the Palatines turned from their fellow Christians to the native savages, and their appeal was not in vain. The Indians gave them permission to settle at Schoharie, and many families removed thither in defiance of the Governor, who was still bent on manufacturing tar and pitch. But the great majority remained in the Hudson valley and eventually built homes on lands which they purchased.

The climate of New York disagreed with Hunter, and his mental depression kept pace with his physical debility. After six years of hopeless effort, he was obliged to admit the failure of his plans to produce naval stores. In 1710 he reported of the locality that it "had the finest air to live upon: but not for me"; again he says that

Sancho Panza is a type for him, since that in spite of every effort to do his duty no dog could be worse treated. It is easy to understand that a member of the Pope-Swift-Bolingbroke circle in England should have found the social atmosphere of early New York far from exhilarating; and it is equally easy to comprehend that the pioneers of the New World resented his mismanagement of the campaign of 1711 against Canada and his assertion of the English Government's right to tax the colonists without the consent of the colonial Governments. But perhaps Hunter and the people appreciated each other more than either realized, for when he took leave in 1719 his words were warmly affectionate and his address embodied the exhortation: "May no strife ever happen amongst you but that laudable emulation who shall approve himself the most zealous servant and most dutiful subject of the best of Princes." And in response to this farewell address the colony of New York assured Governor Hunter that he had governed well and wisely, "like a prudent magistrate, like an affectionate parent," and that the good wishes of his countrymen followed him wherever he went.

It would be pleasant to dwell on this picture of

mutual confidence and regard, but the rude facts of history hurry us on to quite different scenes. William Burnet, son of the Bishop of Salisbury, continued the policy of his predecessor, it is true, and lived on unusually amicable terms with the Assembly. He identified himself with the interests of the province by marrying the daughter of a prosperous Dutch merchant and by prohibiting the fur trade between Albany and Canada; yet even Burnet clashed with the Assembly on occasion. And when after an interval William Cosby became Governor, the worst abuses of executive power returned, fomenting quarrels which reached a climax in the famous Zenger trial.

The truth was that no matter how popular a governor might be, clashes were bound to occur between him and the representatives of the people whom he governed, because they represented divergent interests. The question of revenue was an ever-recurring cause of trouble. Without adequate funds from the home Government, the Governor looked to the Assembly for his salary as well as for grants to carry on the administration of the province. No matter how absolute the authority conferred by his commission and his instructions, the Governor must bow to the lower house of the provincial Legislature, which held the purse strings.

Under Sloughter, Fletcher, Bellomont, and Cornbury the Assembly had voted revenues for a term of years. But when Cornbury appropriated to his own uses £1000 out of the £1800 granted for the defense of the frontiers and when in addition he pocketed £1500 of the funds appropriated for the protection of the mouth of the Hudson, the Assembly grew wary. Thereafter for four successive years it made only annual appropriations, and, wiser still by 1739, it voted supplies only in definite amounts for special purposes. Short-sighted the Assembly often was, sometimes in its parsimony leaving the borders unprotected and showing a disposition to take as much and to give as little as possible — a policy that was fraught with grave peril as the French and Indian War drew on apace.

The growing insubordination of the province gave more than one governor anxious thought. Governor Hunter wrote warningly to friends in England: "The colonies are infants at their mother's breasts and will wean themselves when they become of age." And Governor Clinton was so incensed by the contumacy of the Assembly that he said bluntly: "Every branch of this legislature may be criminal in the eyes of the law, and there is a power able to punish you and that will punish you if you provoke that power to do it by your behaviour. *Otherwise you must think yourselves independent of the crown of Great Britain!*"

CHAPTER XII

THE ZENGER TRIAL

AMONG the children of the Palatines imported by Governor Hunter in 1710 was a lad of thirteen by the name of John Peter Zenger. Instead of proceeding to the Palatine colony, his widowed mother and her little family remained in New York. There Peter was bound apprentice to William Bradford, then a well-known printer, for a term of eight years, at the end of which time he set up an office of his own. He evidently found himself hard pressed for the means of living, since one finds him in 1732 applying to the consistory of the Dutch Church of New York and proposing that, since he had so long played the organ without recompense, he might take up a voluntary subscription from the congregation and that the members of the consistory should head the paper as an example to others. The consistory agreed to allow him provisionally the sum of six pounds, New York currency, to be paid by the church masters and promised that they would speak with him further on the subject of his seeking subscriptions in the congregation, a favor for which John Peter was duly grateful.

Governor William Cosby, as he drove in his coach on a Sunday to Trinity Church, or as he walked in stately raiment, attended by a negro servant who carried his prayer-book on a velvet cushion, could have little dreamed that the young printer striding past him on his way to play the organ in the old Dutch Church was destined to be the instrument of His Excellency's downfall; but the time was not far off when this David, armed only with a blackened type of his printer's form, was to set forth against this Goliath. All flaming convictions have a tendency to cool into cant, and "the Freedom of the Press" has so long been a vote-catching phrase that it is hard nowadays to realize that it was once an expression of an ideal for which men were willing to die but which they scarcely hoped to achieve.

When Colonel Cosby, former Governor of Minorca, came over the seas in 1732, to become Governor of New York, he brought with him a none too savory reputation. All that he seemed

to have learned in his former executive post was
the art of conveying public funds to private uses.
His government in New York sustained his reputation: it was as high-handed as it was corrupt.
He burned deeds and strove to overthrow old land-
patents, in order that fees for new ones might find
their way into his pocket. "Cosby's Manor," a
vast tract of land in the Mohawk Valley, bore testimony to the success of his methods in acquiring
wealth.

Upon the death of Cosby's predecessor, John
Montgomerie, in 1731, Rip van Dam, as president
of the Council, had assumed control of the affairs
of the province until the arrival of the new Governor. At the close of his term, which had lasted a
little more than a year, the Council passed warrants
giving Rip van Dam the salary and the fees of the
office for the time of his service. When Cosby
appeared he produced an order from the King
commanding that the perquisites of the Governor
during the interregnum be equally divided between him and Van Dam. On the authority of
this document, Cosby demanded half of the salary
which Van Dam had received.   "Very well,"
answered the stalwart Dutchman, "but always
provided that you share with me on the same

authority the half of the emoluments which you have received during the same period."

The greedy Governor maintained that this was a very different matter. Nevertheless he was somewhat puzzled as to how to proceed legally with a view to filling his purse. Since he was himself Chancellor, he could not sue in chancery. He did not dare to bring a suit at common law, as he feared that a jury would give a verdict against him. Under these circumstances Cosby took advantage of a clause in the commissions of the judges of the Supreme Court which seemed to constitute them Barons of the Exchequer, and he therefore directed that an action against Van Dam be brought in the name of the King before that court. The Chief Justice, who had held office for eighteen years, was Lewis Morris. Van Dam's counsel promptly took exception to the jurisdiction of the court and Morris sustained their plea, whereupon Cosby removed Morris as Chief Justice. Cosby's party included De Lancey, Philipse, Bradley, and Harrison, while Alexander, Stuyvesant, Livingston, Cadwallader Colden, and most of the prominent citizens, supported Van Dam. The people of New York were now awakening to the fact that this was no petty quarrel between two men as to which should receive the larger share of government moneys, but that it involved the much larger question of whether citizens were to be denied recourse to impartial courts in the defense of their rights.

The only paper published in the province, the *New York Weekly Gazette*, established in 1725, was entirely in Cosby's interest, and the Van Dam party seemed powerless. They determined, however, to strike at least one blow for freedom, and as a first step they established in 1733 a paper known as the *New York Weekly Journal*, to be published by John Peter Zenger, but to be under the control of far abler men. Morris, Alexander, Smith, and Colden were the principal contributors to the new paper, and in a series of articles they vigorously criticized the Governor's administration, particularly his treatment of Van Dam. The Governor and Council in high dudgeon at once demanded the punishment of the publisher. They asked the Assembly to join them in prosecuting Zenger, but the request was laid upon the table. The Council then ordered the hangman to make a public bonfire of four numbers of the *Weekly Journal;* but the mayor and the aldermen declared the order illegal and refused to allow it to be carried out. Accordingly the offending numbers of the *Journal* were burned by a negro slave of the sheriff in the presence of Francis Harrison, the recorder, and some other partizans of Cosby, the magistrates declining to be present at the ceremony. Whatever satisfaction the Governor and his adherents could gain from the burning of these copies of the *Journal* was theirs; but their action served only to make them both more ridiculous and more despicable in the eyes of the people.

Not long after this episode Zenger was arrested upon order of the Council and thrown into the jail, which was at that time in the City Hall on the site of the present United States Sub-Treasury building on Wall Street. Zenger was denied the use of pens, ink, or paper. The grand jury refused to indict him. But Cosby's attorney-general filed an "information" against Zenger for "false, scandalous, malicious and seditious libels."

Public interest was now transferred from Van Dam to Zenger, and the people saw him as their representative, robbed of his right of free speech and imprisoned on an "information" which was in form and substance an indictment without action of a grand jury. Months elapsed while Zenger was kept in prison. His counsel, Smith and Alexander, attacked two judges of the court before which he was to be tried, on the ground that they were irregularly appointed, the commissions of two of them, Chief Justice De Lancey and Judge Philipse, running "during pleasure" instead of "during good behavior" and having been granted by the Governor without the advice or consent of his Council. The anger of the judges thus assailed was expressed by De Lancey, who replied: "You have brought it to that point, gentlemen, that either we must go from the bench or you from the bar," wherewith he summarily ordered the names of the two distinguished lawyers stricken from the list of attorneys.

This was obviously a heavy blow to Zenger, as the only other lawyer of note in New York was retained in the interests of Cosby and his faction. But Zenger's friends never ceased their determined efforts in his behalf, and Smith and Alexander remained active in counsel if not in court. Meanwhile the judges appointed an insignificant attorney, John Chambers by name, to act for Zenger and fancied that their intrigue was sure of success.

The trial came on before the Supreme Court sitting on August 4, 1735, De Lancey acting as Chief Justice, Philipse as second judge, and

Bradley as attorney-general. Chambers pleaded "not guilty" on behalf of his client; but to the throng who crowded the court-room to suffocation, Zenger's case must have looked black indeed. There was no question that he had published the objectionable articles, and according to the English law of the day the truth of a libel could not be set up as a defense. It was even some years later that Lord Mansfield upheld the amazing doctrine that "the greater the truth the greater the libel." A part of the importance of the Zenger trial lies in its sweeping away in this part of the world the possibility of so monstrous a theory.

A great and overwhelming surprise, however, awaited the prosecutors of Zenger. The secret had been well kept and apparently every one was amazed when there appeared for the defense one Andrew Hamilton, a citizen of Philadelphia, of venerable age and the most noted and able lawyer in the colonies. From this moment he became the central figure of the trial and his address was followed with breathless interest. He touched upon his own age and feebleness with consummate tact and dramatic effect:

You see that I labour under the weight of years, and am borne down with great infirmities of body; yet, old and weak as I am, I should think it my duty, if required, to go to the utmost part of the land, where my service could be of use in assisting to quench the flame of prosecutions upon *information* set on foot by the government, to deprive a people of the right of remonstrating (and complaining too) of the arbitrary attempts of men in power. Men who injure and oppress the people under their administration provoke them to cry out and complain, and then make that very complaint the foundation for new oppressions and prosecutions. I wish I could say there were no instances of this kind. But to conclude: the question before the court, and you, gentlemen of the jury, is not of small nor private concern; it is not the cause of a poor printer, nor of New York alone, which you are now trying. No! It may in its consequence affect every freeman that lives under a British government on the main of America! It is the best cause. It is the cause of liberty, and I make no doubt but your upright conduct this day will not only entitle you to the love and esteem of your fellow-citizens, but every man who prefers freedom to a life of slavery will bless and honour you, as men who have baffled the attempt of tyranny, and by an impartial and uncorrupt verdict have laid a noble foundation for securing to ourselves, our posterity, and our neighbors, that to which nature and the laws of our country have given us a right — the liberty both of exposing and opposing arbitrary power . . . by speaking and writing *truth!*

With scathing irony he fell upon the theory that **truth** was no defense for libel:

If a libel is understood in the large and unlimited sense
urged by Mr. Attorney, there is scarce a writing I know
that may not be called a libel, or scarce any person safe
from being called to account as a libeller; for Moses,
meek as he was, libelled Cain, and who is it that has not
libelled the devil? For according to Mr. Attorney, it is
no justification to say that one has a bad name. Echard
has libelled our good King William; Burnet has libelled
among others, King Charles and King James; and
Rapin has libelled them all. How must a man speak or
write, or what must he hear, read, or sing? Or when
must he laugh, so as to be secure from being taken up
as a libeller? I sincerely believe that were some persons
to go through the streets of New York nowadays and
read a part of the Bible, if it were not known to be such,
Mr. Attorney, with the help of his innuendoes, would
easily turn it into a libel. As for instance, the sixteenth
verse of the ninth chapter of Isaiah: *The leaders of the
people cause them to err, and they that are led by them are
destroyed.* But should Mr. Attorney go about to make
this a libel, he would treat it thus: "The leaders of the
people (innuendo, the governor and council of New
York) cause them (innuendo, the people of this province) to err, and they (meaning the people of the
province) are destroyed (innuendo, are deceived into
the loss of their liberty)," which is the worst kind
of destruction. Or, if some person should publicly
repeat, in a manner not pleasing to his betters, the
tenth and eleventh verses of the fifty-sixth chapter of
the same book, there Mr. Attorney would have a large
field to display his skill in the artful application of his
innuendoes. The words are, "His watchmen are all
blind, they are ignorant; yes, they are greedy dogs, that

can never have enough." But to make them a libel, there is according to Mr. Attorney's doctrine, no more wanting but the aid of his skill in the right adapting of his innuendoes. As for instance, "His watchmen (innuendo, the governor's council and Assembly) are blind; they are ignorant (innuendo, will not see the dangerous designs of His Excellency); yea they (meaning the governor and council) are greedy dogs which can never have enough (innuendo, enough of riches and power)."

Thus Hamilton skillfully appealed to the independent principles of the jury. There was no note, satiric, pathetic, or patriotic, which he did not strike. Overwhelmed by the torrent of his eloquence, Bradley, the Attorney-General, scarcely attempted a reply. The Chief Justice stated that the jury might bring in a verdict on the fact of publication and leave it to the Court to decide whether it were libelous. But Hamilton was far too wary to be caught thus. "I know, may it please your Honor," said he, "the jury may do so; but I do likewise know that they may do otherwise. I know they have the right, beyond all dispute, to determine both the law and the fact, and where they do not doubt the law, they ought to do so." Nevertheless the Chief Justice charged the jury:

Gentlemen of the Jury: The great pains Mr. Hamilton has taken, to show you how little regard juries are to pay to the opinion of the judges, and his insisting so much upon the conduct of some judges in trials of this kind, is done, no doubt, with a design that you should take but very little notice of what I might say upon this occasion. I shall, therefore, only observe to you that, as the facts or words in the information are confessed; the only thing that can come in question before you is whether the words set forth in the information, make a libel. And that is a matter of law, no doubt, and which you may leave to the Court.

But the show of authority and the attempt at allurement were all in vain. The jury took but a few moments to deliberate and returned with the verdict of "not guilty." The roar of applause which shook the court-room was more than a tribute to the eloquence of the aged counsel who had accepted an unpopular case without fees because he felt that he was working for the cause of freedom. It was more than a tribute to the poor printer who had risked everything in the same cause. It was the spirit of the barons at Runnymede, of the Long Parliament, of the Revolution of 1688, of Patrick Henry of Virginia when he cried: "Give me liberty or give me death!"

The Court, divided between wrath and surprise, strove to check the wave of applause and threatened with imprisonment the leader of the cheers;

but a son-in-law of ex-Chief Justice Lewis Morris succeeded in making himself heard, and declared that cheers were as lawful there as in Westminster Hall, where they had been loud enough over the acquittal of the seven bishops in 1688. Upon this the applause broke out again, and Hamilton was acclaimed the people's champion. A dinner was given in his honor and the freedom of the city was bestowed upon him. When he entered his barge for the return journey to Philadelphia, flags waved, cannon boomed, and hurrahs resounded from all quarters.

CHAPTER XIII

THE NEGRO PLOTS

As early as the eighteenth century New York had become a cosmopolitan town. Its population contained not only Dutch and English in nearly equal numbers, but also French, Swedes, Jews, Negroes, and sailors, travelers from every land. The settled portion of the city, according to a map of 1729, extended as far north as Beekman Street on the East Side and as far as Trinity Church on the West Side. A few blocks beyond the church lay Old Wind Mill Lane touching King's Farm, which was still open country. Here Broadway shook off all semblance to a town thoroughfare and became a dusty country road, meeting the post-road to Boston near the lower end of the rope walk. "The cittie of New York is a pleasant, well-compacted place," wrote Madam Knight, who journeyed on horseback from Boston over this post-road and who recorded her experiences in an entertaining journal. "The buildings brick generally, very stately and high, though not altogether like ours in Boston. The bricks in some of the houses are of divers coullers and laid in checkers, being glazed look very agreeable. The inside of them are neat to admiration."

Besides its welcoming houses set among spreading trees, New York possessed public buildings of dignity and distinction. There was Trinity Church, whose tall steeple was one of the first landmarks to catch the traveler's eye as he journeyed down the river from Albany. The new City Hall, dating from Bellomont's time and standing on a site at the corner of Wall and Broad Streets, given by Colonel Abraham de Peyster, was also a source of pride. With its substantial wings and arched colonnade in the center it was quite imposing. Here the Assembly, Council, and Court sat. Here, too, were offices and a library. But the cellar was used as a dungeon and the attic as a common prison.

New markets and wharves told of the growing commerce of the city and province. On every hand were evidences of luxurious living. There were taverns and coffee-houses where gold flowed in abundant streams from the pockets of pirates and smugglers, and in the streets crest-emblazoned

family coaches, while sedan chairs were borne by
negro slaves along the narrow brick pathways in
the center of the town. The dress of the people
told the same story of prosperity. The streets
of the fashionable quarter around Trinity Church
were fairly ablaze with gay costumes. Men of
fashion wore powdered wigs and cocked hats, cloth
or velvet coats reaching to the knee, breeches, and
low shoes with buckles. They carried swords,
sometimes studded with jewels, and in their gloved
hands they held snuff-boxes of costly material and
elaborate design. The ladies who accompanied
them were no less gaily dressed. One is described
as wearing a gown of purple and gold, opening over
a black velvet petticoat and short enough to show
green silk stockings and morocco shoes embroidered
in red. Another wore a flowered green and gold
gown, over a scarlet and gold petticoat edged with
silver. Everywhere were seen strange fabrics of
oriental design coming from the holds of mysterious ships which unloaded surreptitiously along the
water front.

The members of one class alone looked on all this
prosperous life with sullen discontent — the negro
slaves whose toil made possible the leisure of their
owners. These strange, uncouth Africans seemed

out of place in New York, and from early times they had exhibited resentment and hatred toward the governing classes, who in turn looked upon them with distrust. This smoldering discontent of the blacks aroused no little uneasiness and led to the adoption of laws which, especially in the cities, were marked by a brutality quite out of keeping with the usual moderation of the colony. When Mrs. Grant wrote later of negro servitude in Albany as "slavery softened into a smile," she spoke in the first place from a narrow observation of life in a cultivated family, and in the second place from scant knowledge of the events which had preceded the kind treatment of the negroes.

In 1684 an ordinance was passed declaring that no negroes or Indian slaves above the number of four should meet together on the Lord's Day or at any other time or at any place except on their master's service. They were not to go armed with guns, swords, clubs, or stones on penalty of ten lashes at the whipping-post. An act provided that no slave should go about the streets after nightfall anywhere south of the Collect without a lighted lantern "so as the light thereof could be plainly seen." A few years later Governor Cornbury ordered the justices of the peace in King's County to seize and

apprehend all negroes who had assembled themselves in a riotous manner or had absconded from
their masters.

In 1712, during the Administration of Governor
Robert Hunter, a group of negroes, perhaps forty
in number, formed a plot which justified the terror
of their masters, though it was so mad that it
could have originated only in savage minds. These
blacks planned to destroy all the white people of
the city, then numbering over six thousand. Meeting in an orchard the negroes set fire to a shed and
then lurked about in the shadows, armed with
every kind of weapon on which they could lay
hands.

As the negroes had expected, all the citizens of
the neighborhood, seeing the conflagration, came
running to the spot to fight the flames. The blacks
succeeded in killing nine men and wounding many
more before the alarm reached the fort. Then of
course the affair ended. The slaves fled to the
forests at the northern end of the island; but the
soldiers stationed sentries and then hunted down
the negroes, beating the woods to be sure that none
escaped. Six of the negroes, seeing that their doom
was sealed, killed themselves, and the fate of the
captives showed that they well knew what mercy

to expect at the hands of the enraged whites. Twenty-one were put to death, one being broken on the wheel and several burned at the stake, while the rest were hanged.

After this experience of the danger attending the holding of slaves, the restrictions upon the negroes grew even more irksome and the treatment they received more that of outcasts. For instance, a slave must be buried by daylight, without pall-bearers and with not more than a dozen negroes present as mourners.

In spite of bright spots in the picture the outlook grew constantly darker; a mistrust ready to develop on slight provocation into terror perturbed the whites; and every rumor was magnified till there reigned a panic as widespread as that caused by the reports of witchcraft in New England. At length in 1741 the storm burst. One March night, while a gale was sweeping the city, a fire was discovered on the roof of the Governor's house in the fort. Church bells sounded the alarm and firemen and engines hurried to the spot; but it was hopeless to try to extinguish the flames, which spread to the chapel and to the office of the secretary over the fort gate, where the records of the colony were stored. The barracks then caught fire, and in a little over an hour everything in the fort was destroyed, the hand-grenades exploding as they caught fire and spreading destruction in every direction.

A month later a fire broke out at night near the Vlei Market. A bucket brigade was formed and the fire was extinguished. On the same night the loft in a house on the west side of the town was found to be in flames, and coals were discovered between two straw beds occupied by a negro. The next day coals were found under the coach-house of John Murray on Broadway, and on the day following a fire broke out again near the Vlei Market. Thus the townsfolk were made certain that an incendiary plot was on foot. Of course every one's thoughts flew to the negro slaves as the conspirators, especially when a Mrs. Earle announced that she had overheard three negroes threatening to burn the town.

The authorities were as much alarmed as the populace and at once leaped to the conclusion that the blame for the incendiarism, of which they scarcely paused to investigate the evidence, was to be divided between the Roman Catholics and the negroes, who without reasonable grounds had so long constituted their chief terror.

The Common Council offered pardon and a reward of one hundred pounds to any conspirator who would reveal the story of the plot and the names of the criminals involved. Under the influence of this offer one Mary Burton, a servant in the employ of Hughson, the tavern-keeper, accused her master, her mistress, their daughter, and a woman of evil reputation known as Peggy Carey, or Kerry, as well as a number of negroes, of being implicated in the plot. She said that the negroes brought stolen goods to the tavern and were protected by Hughson, who had planned with them the burning and plundering of the city and the liberation of the slaves. On this unsupported evidence Peggy Carey and a number of negroes were condemned to execution, and under terror of death, or encouraged by the hope of pardon, these prisoners made numerous confessions implicating one another, until by the end of August twenty-four whites and one hundred and fifty-four negroes had been imprisoned. Four whites, including Hughson and Peggy Carey, were executed; fourteen negroes were burned at the stake; eighteen were hanged, seventy-one transported, and the remainder pardoned or discharged.

Accusations were also made that the Roman

Catholics had stirred up the plot; and persons of reputation and standing were accused of complicity. The effect of the popular panic, which rendered impossible the calm weighing of evidence and extinguished any sense of proportion, is seen in the letters of Governor George Clarke. On June 20, 1741, he writes to the Lords of Trade as follows:

The fatal fire that consumed the buildings in the fort and great part of my substance (for my loss is not less than two thousand pounds), did not happen by accident as I at first apprehended, but was kindled by design, in the execution of a horrid Conspiracy to burn it and the whole town, and to Massacre the people; as appears evidently not only by the Confession of the Negro who set fire to it, in some part of the same gutter where the Plumber was to work, but also by the testimony of several witnesses. How many Conspirators there were we do not yet know; every day produces new discoveries, and I apprehend that in the town, if the truth were known, there are not many innocent Negro men. . . . I do myself the honor to send your Lordships the minutes taken at the tryal of Quack who burned the fort, and of another Negro, who was tryed with him, and their confession at the stake; with some examinations, whereby your Lordships will see their designs; it was ridiculous to suppose that they could keep possession of the town, if they had destroyed the white people, yet the mischief they would have done in pursuit of their intention would nevertheless have been great. . . . Whether, or how far, the hand of popery has been in this hellish conspiracy, I cannot yet discover; but there is room to suspect it, by what two of the Negroes have confessed, viz: that soon after they were spoke to, and had consented to be parties to it, they had some checks of conscience, which they said, would not suffer them to burn houses and kill the White people; whereupon those who drew them into the conspiracy told them, there was no sin or wickedness in it, and that if they would go to Huson's [Hughson's] house, they should find a man who would satisfy them; but they say they would not, nor did go. Margaret Keny [Kerry] was supposed to be a papist, and it is suspected that Huson and his wife were brought over to it. There was in town some time ago a man who is said to be a Romish Priest, who used to be at Huson's but has disappeared ever since the discovery of the conspiracy and is not now to be found.

Later in the summer the Governor recorded his suspicions as follows:

We then thought it [the] Plot was projected only by Huson [Hughson] and the Negroes; but it is now apparent that the hand of popery is in it, for a Romish Priest having been tryed, was upon full and clear evidence convicted of having a deep share in it. . . . Where, by whom, or in what shape this plot was first projected is yet undiscovered; that which at present seems most probable is that Huson, an indigent fellow of a vile character, casting in his thoughts how to mend his circumstances, inticed some Negroes to rob their Masters and to bring the stolen [goods] to him on promise of reward when they were sold; but seeing that by this pilfering trade riches did not flow into him fast enough, and finding the Negroes fit instruments for any villainy, he then fell upon the schemes of burning the fort and town, and murdering the people, as the speediest way to enrich himself and them, and to gain their freedom, for that was the Negroes main inducement. . . . The conspirators had hopes given them that the Spaniards would come hither and join with them early in the Spring; but if they failed of coming, then the business was to be done by the Conspirators without them; many of them were christen'd by the Priest, absolved from all their past sins and whatever they should do in the Plott; many of them sworn by him (others by Huson) to burn and destroy, and to be secret; wherein they were but too punctual; how weak soever the scheme may appear, it was plausible and strong enough to engage and hold the Negroes, and that was all that the Priest and Huson wanted; for had the fort taken fire in the night, as it was intended, the town was then to have been fired in several places at once; in which confusion much rich plunder might have been got and concealed; and if they had it in view too, to serve the enemy, they could not have done it more effectually; for this town being laid in ashes his Majesties forces in the West Indies might have suffered much for want of provisions, and perhaps been unable to proceed upon any expedition or piece of service from whence they might promise themselves great rewards; I doubt the business is pretty nigh at an end, for since the Priest has been apprehended, and some more white men named, great industry has been used throughout the town to discredit the witnesses and prejudice the people against them; and I am told it has had in a great measure its intended effect; I am sorry for it, for I do not think we are yet got near the bottom of it, where I doubt the principal conspirators lie concealed.

With the collapse of the excitement through its own excess, ends the history of the great negro "plot." Whether it had any shadow of reality has never been determined. Judge Horsmanden, who sat as one of the justices during the trials growing out of the so-called plots, compiled later a record of examinations and alleged confessions whereby he sought to justify the course of both judges and juries; but the impression left by his report is that panic had paralyzed the judgment of even the most honest white men, while among the negroes a still greater terror, combined with a wave of hysteria, led to boundless falsification and to numberless unjustified accusations.

CHAPTER XIV

THE story of the French and Indian wars on our border does not fall within the scope of this chronicle; but in order to understand the development of New York we must know something of the conditions which prevailed in the province during that troubled epoch. The penurious policy pursued by the Dutch and continued by the English left the colony without defenses on either the northern or southern boundaries. For a long time the settlers found themselves bulwarked against the French on the north by the steadfast friendship of the "Six Nations," comprising the Mohawks, the Oneidas, the Onondagas, the Cayugas, the Senecas, and the Tuscaroras; but at last these trusty allies began to feel that the English were not doing their share in the war. The lack of military preparation in New York was inexcusable. The niggardliness of the Assembly alienated successive governors and justified Clinton's assertion: "If you deny me the necessary supplies all my endeavors must become fruitless. I must wash my own hands and leave at your doors the blood of innocent people."

When the Indians under the leadership of the French actually took the warpath, the colonists at last awoke to their peril. Upon call of Lieutenant-Governor De Lancey, acting under instructions of the Lords of Trade, all the colonies north of the Potomac except New Jersey sent commissioners to a congress at Albany in June, 1754, to plan measures of defense and of alliance with the Six Nations.

Albany was still a placid little Dutch town. Mrs. Grant of Laggan in Scotland, who visited Albany in her girlhood, wrote of it afterward with a gentle suavity which lent glamour to the scenes which she described. She pictures for us a little town in which every house had its garden at the rear and in front a shaded stoop with seats on either side where the family gathered to enjoy the twilight. "Each family had a cow, fed in a common pasture at the end of the town. In the evening they returned all together, of their own accord, with their tinkling bells hung at their necks, along the wide and grassy street, to their wonted sheltering trees, to be milked. At one door were young matrons, at another the elders of the people, at a third the youths and maidens, gaily chatting or singing together, while the children played around the trees, or waited by the cows for the chief ingredient of their frugal supper, which they generally ate sitting on the steps in the open air."

The court-house of Albany to which the commissioners journeyed by boat up the Hudson, is described by Peter Kalm, a Swedish traveler and scientist, as a fine stone building by the riverside, three stories high with a small steeple containing a bell, and topped by a gilt ball and weather-vane. From the engraved print which has come down to us, it seems a barren barrack of a building with an entrance quite inadequate for the men of distinction who thronged its halls on this memorable occasion.

In this congress at Albany, Benjamin Franklin from Pennsylvania and William Johnson of New York were the dominating figures. The famous plan of union which Franklin presented has sometimes made historians forget the services rendered by this redoubtable Colonel Johnson at a moment when the friendship of the Six Nations was hanging in the balance. Though gifts had been prepared and a general invitation had been sent, only a hundred and fifty warriors appeared at Albany and they held themselves aloof with a distrust that was almost contempt. "Look at the French!" exclaimed Hendrick, the great chief of the Mohawks. "They are men. They are fortifying everywhere; but, we are ashamed to say it, you are all like women — bare and open without any fortifications." In this crisis all the commissioners deferred to William Johnson as the one man who enjoyed the complete confidence of the Six Nations. It was he who formulated the Indian policy of the congress.

He had been born in Ireland. His mother was Anne Warren, sister to Captain Peter Warren, who "served with reputation" in the Royal Navy and afterward became Knight of the Bath and Vice-Admiral of the Red Squadron of the British Fleet. Captain Warren was less than a dozen years older than his nephew, whom he regarded with affectionate interest. He described him as "a spritely boy well grown of good parts and keen wit but most onruly and streperous," and the sailor added: "I see the making of a strong man. I shall keep my weather eye on the lad."

The result of this observation was so favorable

that the captain, who was on station in America, sent for William Johnson to come out and aid him in the development of a real estate venture. A large tract of land near the Mohawk River had come into Warren's possession, and as a sailor Warren naturally found difficulty in superintending land at what was then a week's journey from the seacoast. "Billy" was his choice as an assistant, and the boy, who was then twenty-three years old, left the Old World and in 1738 reached the new plantation where his life-work lay before him. For this he was admirably equipped by his Irish inheritance of courage, tact, and humor, by his study of English law, and by a facility in acquiring languages which enabled him to master the Mohawk tongue in two years after his arrival in New York.

The business arrangement between Captain Warren and his nephew provided that Johnson should form a settlement on his uncle's land known as Warrensbush, at the juncture of Schoharie Kill and the Mohawk, that he should sell farms, oversee settlers, clear and hedge fields, "girdle" trees (in order to kill them and let in the sun), purchase supplies, and in partnership with Warren establish a village store to meet the necessities of the new colonists and to serve as a trading-station with the Indians. In compensation for his services he was to be allowed to cultivate a part of the land for himself, though it is hard to imagine what time or strength could have been left for further exertions after the fulfillment of the onerous duties marked out for him.

A few years after his arrival at Warrensbush he married a young Dutch or German woman named Catherine Weisenberg, perhaps an indentured servant whose passage had been prepaid on condition of service in America. Little is known of the date or circumstances of this marriage. It is certain only that after a few years Catherine died, leaving three children, to whom Johnson proved a kind and considerate father, in spite of an erratic domestic career which involved his taking as the next head of his household Caroline, niece of the Mohawk chief Hendrick, and later Molly Brant, sister of the Indian, Joseph Brant.

Molly Brant, by whom Johnson had eight children, was recognized as his wife by the Indians, while among Johnson's English friends she was known euphemistically as "the brown Lady Johnson." She presided over his anomalous household with dignity and discretion; but it is noticeable that Johnson, who was so willing to defy public opinion in certain matters, was sufficiently conventional in others, as we learn from a description of the daily life of the legitimate daughters of the house. While Mohawk chiefs, Oneida braves, Englishmen of title, and distinguished guests of every kind thronged the mansion, and while the little half-breed children played about the lawns and disported themselves on the shores of Kayaderosseras Creek close at hand, "the young ladies" lived in almost conventual seclusion.

The grim baronial mansion where this mixed household made its dwelling for many years, was called variously Mount Johnson, Castle Johnson, and Fort Johnson. It was built in 1742 with such massive walls that the house is still standing in the town of Amsterdam. In 1755, when the Indian peril loomed large on the horizon, the original defenses were strengthened, a stockade was built as a further protection, and from this time on it was called Fort Johnson.

Owing perhaps to Johnson's precautions and the Indian's knowledge of his character, the fort was not attacked and its owner continued to dwell in the house until 1762, when, having become one of the richest men in the colony, he built on a tract of land in Johnstown a more ambitious, and, it is to be hoped, a more cheerful mansion known as Johnson Hall. This house was built of wood with wings of stone, pierced at the top for muskets. On one side of the house lay a garden and nursery described as the pride of the surrounding country. Here Johnson lived with an opulence which must have amazed the simple settlers around him, especially those who remembered his coming to the colony as a poor youth less than thirty years earlier. He had in his service a secretary, a physician, a musician who played the violin for the entertainment of guests, a gardener, a butler, a waiter named Pontiach, of mixed negro and Indian blood, a pair of white dwarfs to attend upon himself and his friends, an overseer, and ten or fifteen slaves.

This retinue of servants was none too large to cope with the unbounded hospitality which Johnson dispensed. A visitor reports having seen at the Hall from sixty to eighty Indians at one time lodging under tents on the lawn and taking their meals from tables made of pine boards spread under the trees. On another occasion, when Sir William called a council of the Iroquois at Fort Johnson, a thousand natives gathered, and Johnson's neighbors within a circuit of twenty miles were invited to assist in the rationing of this horde of visitors. The landholders along the Mohawk might well have been glad to share the burden of Sir William's tribal hospitality, since its purpose was as much political as social and its results were of endless benefit to the entire colony.

At last the Indians had found a friend, a white man who understood them and whom they could understand. He was honest with them and therefore they trusted him. He was sympathetic and therefore they were ready to discuss their troubles freely with him. As an Indian of mixed blood declared to the Governor at Albany in speaking of Sir William: "His knowledge of our affairs, our laws, and our language made us think he was not like any other white but an Indian like ourselves. Not only that; but in his house is an Indian woman, and his little children are half-breed as I am."

The English therefore were peculiarly fortunate in finding at the most critical stage of their political dealings with the Indians a representative endowed with the wisdom and insight of Sir William Johnson. Unlike the French, he did not strive to force an alien form of worship upon this primitive people. Unlike the Dutch, he insisted that business should be carried on as honestly with the natives as with the white men. Unlike his fellow-countrymen, he constantly urged adequate preparation for war on the part of the English and demanded that they should bear their share of the burden. In a written report at the Albany congress he strongly recommended that inasmuch as the Six Nations, owing to their wars with the French, had fallen short both in hunting and planting, they should be provided with food from the English supplies. Finally he testified to the sincerity of his convictions by going to the war himself and rendering valuable service first as colonel and later as major-general. After the Battle of Lake George, Johnson was knighted by the King and received a grant of £5000 from Parliament. In the same year he was appointed by the Crown "Agent and Sole Superintendent of the Six Nations and other northern Indians" inhabiting British territory north of the Carolinas and the Ohio River.

Johnson is described by one who saw him about this time or somewhat earlier as a man of commanding presence, only a little short of six feet in height, "neck massive, broad chest and large limbs, great physical strength, the head large and shapely, countenance open and beaming with good nature, eyes grayish black, hair brown with tinge of auburn." His activity took every form and was exerted in every direction. His documents and correspondence number over six thousand and fill twenty-six volumes preserved in the State Library. Nor did these represent his chief activities. He was constantly holding councils with the native tribes either at Fort Johnson or at the Indian camps. It was he who kept the Mohawks from joining in Pontiac's conspiracy which swept the western border; it was he who negotiated the famous treaty at Fort Stanwix in 1768. In the midsummer of 1774 he succumbed to an old malady after an impassioned address to six hundred Iroquois gathered at Johnson Hall.

He was one of the fortunate few whose characters and careers fit exactly. He found scope for every power that he possessed and he won great rewards. His tireless energy expressed itself in cultivating thousands of acres and in building houses, forts, and churches. He dipped a lavish hand into his abundant wealth and scattered his gold where it was of the greatest service. He loved hospitality and gathered hundreds round his board. He was a benevolent autocrat and nations bowed to his will. He paid homage to his King, and died cherishing the illusion of the value of prerogative. He was fortunate in his death as in his life, for he was spared the throes of the mighty changes already under way, when the King's statue should be pulled down to be melted into bullets, when New York should merge her identity in the Union of States, and when the dwellers along the banks of the Hudson and its tributaries should call themselves no longer Dutch or English but Americans.

BIBLIOGRAPHICAL NOTE

THE student who has the courage to delve in the *Documents relative to the Colonial History of the State of New York*, the *Documentary History of the State of New York*, the ecclesiastical records, the pioneer journals, and the minutes of early city councils, will not only reach the fundamental authorities on the history of the settlers on the Hudson, but will find many interesting incidents of which the dull titles give no promise.

If the reader prefer to follow a blazed trail, he will find a path marked out for him in reliable works such as *The History of New Netherland* by E. B. O'Callaghan, 2 vols. (1855), *The History of the State of New York* by J. R. Brodhead, 2 vols. (1871), *The Narratives of New Netherland*, admirably edited by J. F. Jameson (1909), *New York*, a condensed history by E. H. Roberts (1904), John Fiske's *Dutch and Quaker Colonies in America*, 2 vols. (1899), and William Smith's *History of the Late Province of New York* (first published in 1757 and still valuable).

Many histories of New York City have been written to satisfy the general reader. Among the larger works are Mrs. M. J. Lamb's *History of the City of New York*, 2 vols. (1877; revised edition, 1915, in 3 vols.), Mrs. Schuyler Van Rensselaer's *History of the City of New York in the Seventeenth Century*, 2 vols. (1909),

James G. Wilson's *Memorial History of the City of New York*, 4 vols. (1892), and *Historic New York*, 2 vols. (edited by M. W. Goodwin, A. C. Royce, and Ruth Putnam, 1912). Theodore Roosevelt has written a single volume on New York for the *Historic Towns* series (1910). In his *New Amsterdam and its People* (1902), J. H. Innes has brought together valuable studies of the social and topographical features of the town under Dutch and early English rule. I. N. P. Stokes's *Iconography of Manhattan Island* (1915) is calculated to delight the soul of the antiquarian.

One who wishes to turn to the lighter side of provincial life will find it set forth in attractive volumes such as *Colonial Days in Old New York* by A. M. Earle (1915), *The Story of New Netherland* by W. E. Griffis (1909), *In Old New York* by T. A. Janvier (1894), and the *Goede Vrouw of Mana-ha-ta* by M. K. Van Rensselaer (1898).

Most rewarding perhaps of all sources are those dealing with the biographies of the prominent figures in the history of the State, since in them we find the life of the times illustrated and personalized. E. M. Bacon in his *Henry Hudson* (1907) gives us a picture of the great mariner and the difficulties against which he strove. The *Van Rensselaer-Bowier Manuscripts*, edited by A. J. F. Van Laer (1908) show us through his personal letters the Patroon of the upper Hudson and make us familiar with life on his estates. J. K. Paulding in *Affairs and Men of New Amsterdam in the Time of Governor Peter Stuyvesant* (1843) makes the town-dwellers equally real to us, while W. L. Stone's *Life and Times of Sir William Johnson*, 2 vols. (1865), shows us the pioneer struggles in the Mohawk Valley. In the English *State Trials* compiled by T. B. Howells, 34 vols. (1828), we read the story of the famous pirate Captain Kidd, and find it more interesting than many a work of fiction.

Among the autobiographical accounts of colonial life the most entertaining are *The Memoirs of an American Lady* by A. M. Grant (1809), *A Two Years' Journal in New York, etc.* by Charles Wolley (1902), and *The Private Journal of Sarah Kemble Knight*, the record of a journey from Boston to New York in 1704 (1901).

Further bibliographical references will be found appended to the articles on *Hudson River, New York*, and *New York (City)*, in *The Encyclopædia Britannica*, 11th edition.

INDEX

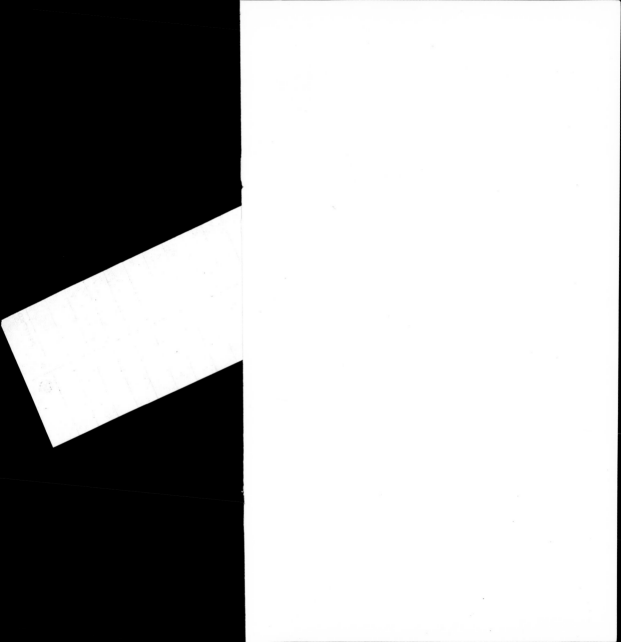

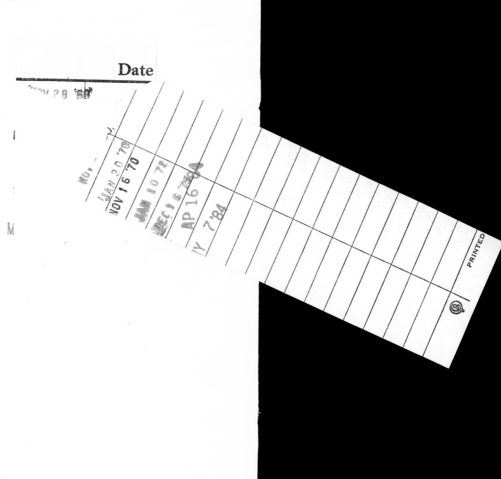